My Life
and
Adventures

James Scott Skinner

City of Aberdeen

in association with

Wallace Music

First published in 1994
by
City of Aberdeen, Arts and Recreation Division,
Central Library, Rosemount Viaduct, Aberdeen,
Scotland, AB9 1GU.

in association with

Wallace Music,
169 Main Street, Pathhead, Midlothian, Scotland,
EH37 5SQ.

FS SKI
1001143

Cover illustration taken from James Scott Skinner
music manuscript of the tune *The Submarine*.
Rear cover photograph courtesy of North Scotland
Museum Service.

ISBN 0-946-920-10 9

Layout and typesetting by Wallace Music.
Printed by BPC-AUP Aberdeen Ltd.

Contents

Photo Morgan, Aberdeen.

To R. Murdoch Lawrance.
from his esteemed friend'.
J. Scott Skinner.

Banchead. 28.8. 1923.

Introduction

The year prior to the publication of this book, 1993, marked the 150th anniversary of the birth of James Scott Skinner. He is one of the all-time greats of Scottish fiddle music as both a performer and as a prolific composer of tunes. Skinner's approach to his native music transcends the traditional approach. Following his very early days as a traditional fiddler, playing by ear, he then received tuition in classical technique which allowed him to set even higher standards as a performer. Something which perhaps tends to be forgotten is that Skinner went beyond the merely traditional approach to fiddle playing, not only in technique, but also in performance. From humble beginnings as a dancing master he ended up playing to vast audiences at places like the London Palladium and also as part of variety entertainments, sharing the bill with the likes of Sir Harry Lauder.

Skinner made a conscious decision to play music in the Scottish idiom, although he did perform other pieces, and dressed the part in kilt and associated regalia. He composed over six hundred tunes, published as sheet music and in a number of larger collections. The tunes vary widely in quality, from the average to the exceptional, many tunes of enduring popularity remaining in the repertoires of fiddlers to the present day. We are lucky that Skinner lived long enough to see the introduction of recording, and some of his performances, admittedly at the end of his career, have been preserved. These give a greater understanding of his technique and powerful playing.

In researching a book on fiddler James Hill, I became intrigued by mentions in various footnotes and bibliographies of Skinner's autobiography. I knew that Skinner had played and had included in one of his published collections *Earl Grey,* a strathspey composed by Hill, and was eager to establish whether or not there might be any references to Hill in the autobiography. I was disappointed to find that there was no information but as compensation I soon became immersed in Skinner's own story.

The autobiography was published towards the end of his life. It appeared as series of articles in twelve weekly instalments in *The People's Journal* commencing on Saturday 3rd February, 1923 and ending on 21st April. It was entitled *My Life and Adventures* and the first instalment was accompanied by a 16 page supplement *Scott Skinner's Book of Selected National Songs.* The autobiography is a wonderful snapshot of the times, (selective) history of Skinner's career and insight into his music. He does not necessarily appear as one of the most modest of men and was an inveterate name-dropper. Nevertheless he took his art seriously and wished to be remembered by some of his better compositions. A wish which has been fulfilled. It is interesting, reading through his tales that a musicians life on the road has, in essence, changed little since his day!

By making the autobiography available again, it is hoped that it will provide a useful background to an understanding of Skinner and his place in Scottish music. Apart from that, it is hoped that it will provide an enjoyable read—some good gossip, tales and flavour of a passed era. Editorial interference has been minimal. Each of the chapters in this book corresponds to one of the original weekly newspaper instalments. The original spelling and punctuation has been retained, along with such conventions of the time as writing McHardy as M'Hardy.

The illustrations are reproduced from copies in the original articles which are in a scrapbook compiled by James Murdoch Henderson, now in the possession of Aberdeen Central

Library. A problem for non-Scots readers may be encountered by some of the Scots words and renderings of dialect in the text. The thought of having to try and produce a glossary proved too fraught with difficulty and I have therefore taken the easy option and would refer readers in any difficulty to consult *The Concise Scots Dictionary*, editor Mairi Robertson, and published by Aberdeen University Press, 1985.

Murdoch Henderson's scrapbook, referred to above, also contains numerous other non-autobiographical cuttings concerning Skinner. Therefore, in an attempt to complete the story, some of these cuttings are reproduced in the appendix of the present book. These give an account of his ill-fated trip to America in 1926, the announcement of his death, obituary and account of the funeral. There is also an assessment of his achievements by a friend, George Riddell, an account of the sale of Skinner's fiddle and other possessions, and finally the moves to erect a suitable memorial at Aberdeen's Allenvale Cemetery. Also interspersed are copies of some posters and concert programmes held by Aberdeen Central Library.

Like any autobiography, Skinner's story is selective and we must await a definitive biography. Hopefully this present book will help stimulate further interest and debate not just concerning Skinner and his music, but Scottish fiddle music in general.

The publication of this book could not have been achieved without the help and encouragement of a number of people and institutions. I wish to convey my heartfelt thanks to John Junner, the ever helpful staff at the National Library of Scotland, Edinburgh, my wife Kate, my partner at Wallace Music, Noel Chidwick, for all his efforts, ScotSys Computer Systems, Edinburgh, and the City of Aberdeen Central Library and, in particular, Jim Pratt for helping to bring this project to fruition. Thank you one and all.

"Lang may your elbuck jink and diddle."

Graham Dixon
Pathhead, Midlothian
February 1994

One

My Family and Childhood Days—Learning the Fiddler's Trade

IT HAS BEEN SAID OF ME THAT I was born with a pen in my ear and a fiddle-stick in my hand, and that I have been getting younger ever since!

While very much doubting these little details of my precocity, I believe there is something in the latter part of the compliment. A woman, they say, is only as old as she looks, and a man as old as he feels. In my eightieth year, when I still have the honour of stringing my beloved fiddle for the entertainment of an appreciative public, I can truthfully say that I feel to-day as young as ever I felt. Mine was for long a strenuous, uphill fight. Tragedy frequently enwrapped me in her chilling mantle, but I have survived, and now, with an honoured niche in the annals of Scottish music indubitably vouchsafed to me, I am young and happy once more.

The sweet, sylvan village of Banchory, on beautiful Deeside, was the setting of my nativity. The house in which I spent my boyhood is no more, but, as a reminder of my many juvenile delinquencies, the old birch tree, up which I used to scamper to escape my maternal Nemesis, still stands in Watson Street.

My father, William Skinner, who originally followed the vocation of a gardener, died while I was still in "lang claes," when, to be exact, I was only eighteen months old. At the time of his death my father was making his livelihood by teaching dancing, and a precarious pursuit it must have been in those days, for I was born, as they say in the north, "wi' mair feet than stockin's."

1

My father's adoption of dancing as a profession was the result of an accident, which incapacitated him for his work as a gardener. In those early days shooting at marriages was considered a necessary part of the celebrations. My father, ever cheerful, active, and sociable and true to old nuptial convention, was blazing away in honour of a wedding party, when the bursting of his firelock deprived him of three of the fingers of his left hand.

A Plucky Parent

Already a skilled amateur in fiddling and dancing, it occured to him that, with his usefulness as a gardener destroyed, he could not do better than devote his musical and terpsichorean talents to keeping the proverbial wolf from the door.

Nothing daunted by the loss of three fingers, my father, who must have been a man of indomitable courage and filled with sturdy Scottish independence, set himself the task of relearning the fiddle vice-versa—that is to say, bowing with the left hand and fingering with the right. A friend kindly helped to solve the problem by transposing a fiddle, and after much experimenting my father found that with the aid of a loop attached to the fiddle he was able to hold and manipulate the bow with his left hand.

In time, by dint of great pluck and perseverance, he became an expert fiddler and the most famous dancing master on Deeside. I remember as a boy speaking to men who had heard my father play after his accident, and their verdict was that the "transposition" was no misfortune, for my father

Banchory—Mr Scott Skinner's birth-place

2

had played even better than in the orthodox or natural method.

At all events, "Dancie" Skinner, as my father was familiarly called, subsequently attended many a wedding feast and many a dance, and obliged with less dangerous accompaniments than the reports of guns and pistols.

My father, I may add, was not only a first-class teacher of dancing, but a first-class performer when dancing was DANCING.

My mother remarried when I was still a little lad. This second adventure on the fickle sea of matrimony proved unhappy, and one by one the family by her first husband, of whom I was the youngest, left the old home.

Of my mother, despite her rigid belief in the scriptural adage that who spareth the rod spoileth the child, I have nought but the tenderest and sweetest of memories. A deep thinker, if not actually gifted with a smattering of the second-sight, my mother, it was well known locally, was addicted to "moralisin' up th' lum," in which connection I recollect a rather prescient remark she made to me when I must have been not more than eight years old. "Jimmie," said she, "gin ye live lang eneuch we'll be seein' the carriages gaun ower Union Brig (Aberdeen) wantin' horses." Candidly, my little mind concluded that my mother was going wrong in the "tap storey," but when readers recollect that even horse-drawn tramcars were not in vogue in Aberdeen in those days, it will be admitted that her prophecy was intelligent, if not remarkable.

My First Theft

If my readers are not impatient of these stories of my early days (it does my auld he'rt guid tae think an' write aboot them!), I will tell the simple tale of how I committed my first and, I believe, my only theft since I was born. (Ahem!)

Next me in the parish school sat a loon of the same age who had a distinct talent for humorous draughtsmanship, and who, if he were available to-day, would, I am sure, be heartily welcomed in the columns of the *People's Journal*. Without a smile or remark he would dash off in school the funniest cartoon of a pig imaginable, and I would be unable to resist the risible provocation. The unfortunate sequel for me was that the schoolmaster, a regular martinet, restored solemnity to my youthful countenance by the application of a cane to the hinder end of my anatomy.

You may wonder why these incidents "gone and done with long ago and far away" remain so clearly in my memory, but, as other people will confirm, while the passage of time somewhat tends to obliterate the happenings of middle life, the events of boyhood and adolescence get bolder and bolder in relief.

But to the story of my first theft. One day my cartoonist companion and I decided to go on a bird "pinking" expedition, if the material for the necessary slings could be procured. Passing through the village together, inspiration dawned on my crony, who, pointing to an unfinished shoe in the local cobbler's shop, suggested I should annex it for our purpose. Considering it was my first adventure of the kind, I was much too prompt to oblige. Adjourning to the Monument Wood, we cut the shoe into strips, fashioned out the required slings, and proceeded to pitch stones at the feathered songsters as merrily as did David at Goliath.

The advent of the local policeman, who had been apprised of the theft of the shoe, put an abrupt end to our frolics. As is always the case, one sin leads to another and (shades of George Washington!) I followed up my first theft with my first falsehood —for the pair of us, thinking ourselves ever so cute, supplied the "Bobby" with wrong names and addresses, forgetful of the fact that Banchory was not London or Glasgow, or even Aberdeen. To cut a long story short, my mother soon got to know of my misbehaviour, and a resounding spanking with the then popular weapon of chastisement, the "broom cow" (a stick cut from the wild broom bush), ere I went to bed, taught me how hard is the way of the transgressor.

Working as a Vamper

I could tell many more memorable incidents of those days, but I must get on with the narrative as it relates to my performances with the fiddle. I could not have been more than six years of age when my brother Sandy took in hand to teach me the fiddle, and, without implying any disrespect to his memory, he was the most rigorous of taskmasters. Looking back on those days, I sometimes marvel that, when left to my own resources, a reactionary revulsion of feeling did not make me eschew the violin for all time. But, despite the grim school in which I was reared, my love for music, and particularly the music of my own country, was deep and innate and strong enough to survive the humiliating punishment I received because of my alleged lack of "glegness in th' uptak'."

Sandy, I should explain, taught me by ear, and it was not till some years later, when I was with Dr.Mark's Little Men—to which musical combination I will refer later—that I learned the theory of music.

With the view to assisting Sandy at dances, I also received simple instruction in the art of vamping on the 'cello, which in those days was called the "bass fiddle," and was transported from place to place in a green baize bag.

4

Our family fortunes at this time were in a pretty bad way, and once Sandy was satisfied (and he was seldom satisfied with anything!) that I could vamp with some degree of efficiency, I trotted out along with him to barn and bothy dances in the neighbourhood to add my little quota to the family exchequer.

Then I went into the employment of Peter Milne, who, in my opinion, was one of the grandest strathspey players that ever graced Scotland, and probably the finest native musician of any country in the world. He was a genius and a great preserver of the finest of the old Scottish

Peter Milne, a famous fiddler of earlier days, who employed Scott Skinner as a boy.

melodies, and a leader of the progressives among strathspey exponents. Jamie Allan, of Forfar, a contemporary, was another of the same type, though not quite up to Peter's standard. My brother Sandy was also powerful, but rougher than either Peter or Jamie. Peter Milne's tunes are finely constructed, his best being a valse, *Pride o' the Dee*. Ilka street fiddler in those days played it.

Peter, like my brother Sandy, made his living—a meagre existence it was—by fiddling at dances in barns, bothies, and lofts in the Deeside district. The pay I received from him at the outset was 5s. per month, irrespective of the number of appearances or hours I put in.

Slept While Playing

Looking back on those hard times, I often wonder how I, a boy of eight or nine years, survived the physical strain and the loss of sleep which my duties with the band occasioned. It was nothing unusual for Peter and me to trudge eight or ten weary miles on a slushy wet night in order to fulfil a barn engagement.

I remember getting back from such a tramp about five o'clock in the morning. So tired was I that when I got to the door, dragging, rather than carrying, my bass fiddle, I had neither the strength nor the will power to lift the latch and enter. I must have been in a subconcious state, for when my mother opened the door about seven I fell right through the doorway, and lay helpless at her feet. I had been sleeping against the door, in a half-standing, half-leaning posture for two hours at least. Some there may be who will be inclined to doubt the truth of this story, but were my poor mother alive she would verify the facts. There were times even when I slept over the bass fiddle at dances, and kept up the vamping subconciously.

On the whole, however, I must say I greatly enjoyed my trips with Peter, who, in his own way, was practically a father to me, and, moreover, at whatever dance I happened to be playing, I was always lionised to a great extent. Pity may have been the inspiring motive of much of the kindness shown me by the country dancers, but I was too young to inquire into the psychology of their actions, and the sweeties with which they filled my pockets to overflowing were appreciated and devoured.

To readers whose knowledge of dancing premises is confined to the ultra-modern "Palais de Dance" of to-day, a description of the conditions that prevailed in my young days should not be without interest.

The barns in which the dancing took place had earthen floors, and were not always quite level. Planks laid on sacks of corn turned on their sides formed the sitting accommodation. Tallow dips mounted on wooden brackets on the walls supplied the lighting, candles not being introduced until about ten years after the period of which I am writing.

The preliminary arrangements were made in the neighbouring farmhouse by a Committee (pronounced Cohmittee) who generally saw that a gallon of whisky was included in the refreshments. The way in which the dancers divided themselves according to sex was reminiscent of a Jewish synagogue, the males sitting on one side of the barn and the females on the other, but once they were all on the floor, the parallel to a Hebrew place of worship was dispelled. The dances of those days were not decorous, let alone sanctimonious.

"Belle of the Ball"

Stewards went around at a suitable interval (generally when the "cratur" had made the dancing gallants amiable) and took up a "lawin'" (collection) to defray the expenses. Men were expected to contribute not less than sixpence, and hauflins threepence, the "fair sex" getting in free.

After several hours dancing, refreshments were served, generally about midnight. These consisted of ginger wine for the ladies and whisky "toddy" for the men. Bread and cheese were carried round and served from a riddle, which was made presentable by a wide white cloth.

Musicians at the far end of the barn extemporised a platform out of the fanner. The orchestra generally consisted of small fiddle, bass fiddle ('cello) for vamping, and an octavo flute.

Outside the barn an old woman, whose tallow dip was more often unlit than lit owing to the wind, sold delightful confections in the form of conversation lozenges inscribed with various terms of endearment. This old woman, by some law which, although unwritten, was as unalterable as those of the Medes and Persians, was denied admission to the barn, and I used to feel very sorry for her when I saw her selling her wares out in the bitter cold, and not infrequently in blinding snow. The sweeties she sold at a groat (4d) per lb., were good value, I assure you.

When it is pointed out that the honour of "belle of the ball" in those days went to the girl who could, at the end of the evening's frivoity, show the greatest number of confections presented by admiring gallants, it will be seen that the old woman was bound to do a roaring trade, compensating her somewhat for the discomforts of her stance. Many of the lasses, as a matter of fact, had quite a task in carrying home their "birn" of sweeties, and I used to think that a pair of scales, as against a laborious count, would have been the more expeditious method of deciding the "belle of the ball."

During the evening a selected few were invited round to the farmhouse to have tea. The honour of being thus "bidden" was highly prized and much sought after. Those thus marked out and favoured considered themselves of "The Elite," for even in those rough times "swank" and "side" were omnipresent at social functions.

About four o'clock in the morning the ball broke up, and many of the lady dancers had to trudge home a distance of from eight to ten miles, and of course, their chiels would have to perform double the distance at least. Truly they took their pleasure seriously when I was a boy.

Peter Milne, who used to say that he was "that fond o' ma fiddle I could sit in the inside o't an look oot," was one of the most original characters I ever knew, but his improvidence was largely responsible for his undoing. He was a native of Tarland, and for power in playing a strathspey few, if any, could equal him. My brother Sandy was said to closely rival him, and was incidentally declared to be a much greater player than he.

The Tragedy of Peter

Peter, despite his failings, rose fairly high in his profession. He was leader of the orchestras (in succession) at the Gaiety and Prince's Theatres, Edinburgh, and at M'Gork's Theatre in Leith. When evil days arrived, he, along with Willie Grant, a blind harmonium player, took to playing their instruments for charitable coppers on the ferryboats that plied between Burntisland and Queensferry before the Forth Bridge was built. The completion and opening of this wonder of the world put Peter once more on the "rocks," and he returned to Aberdeen, where the foolhardy prank of an intimate, in pulling away a chair as Peter went to sit down, disabled him for the rest of his days—ten years to be exact—which he spent in a hospital in his beloved Bon Accord.

I remember one occasion when Peter and I were between Corse and Lumphanan, on the way to an engagement, Peter said to me—"Man, Jimmie, I want snuff an' I want my opium. Wid ye gang on tae Lumphanan tae th' druggist's an' get them for me?" I consented, and he handed me a paper with his order written on it and the requisite money enclosed. Then he gave me a sixpence, saying—"That'll get a piece tae yersel, Jimmie."

I covered the three miles to Lumphanan as quickly as I could, and, as chemists weren't so particular or so restricted in those days as they are now, I easily obtained Peter's order. When I saw the druggist putting the snuff in paper, says I to myself—"Maybe Peter'll let it fall and lose a' the snuff," so the bright idea of buying Peter a snuff-box entered my head. This I did with the sixpence he had given me to get a piece.

"Whaur's yer piece?" said Peter on my return, and I handed him the opium and snuff-box containing the snuff.

"Awa' ye saft-he'rted loon," says he, "tae buy a snuff-mill an' ye hungry!" And he burst into tears. Such was the man.

Peter was an inveterate opium addictee. He bought it in solid form and chewed it, and if he chanced to be on the way to a concert, after he had chewed some of the stuff, from being dull and morose, he would become bright and optimistic.

"Jimmie," he would exclaim excitedly, "D'ye see them? Th' front seats are a' full up, an' th' hale place is crooded. Laddie, we're gaun tae hae a great hoose this nicht."

Later in life I met Peter in Aberdeen, just as he was preparing for a flitting, which all through his career was quite a passion with him. He never stayed long in one house.

"Peter," said I, "are ye flittin' again?"

"Aye," was the curt reply.

"Whaur are ye gane tae bide?"

"Oh, I'm gaun up tae th' East End."

"An' whit wey are ye gaun there?"

"Oh, tae be nearer my work."

"An' whaur are ye workin'?"

"Lord, man," he exclaimed, "I hinna got a job yet!"

A Boy's Invention

When I was about nine years of age my mother decided to send me to Aberdeen so that I could attend Connell's School, which was then in Princes

Street. It was arranged that I was to reside with my married sister, Mrs Dalgarno, who lived at 22 Frederick Street, which was quite close to the school. My sister, who had two of a family at the time, lived on the second storey, and I remember that on a certain washing day she asked me to rock the cradle containing my little niece (now a married woman with a large family) while she put "th' fite things in th' b'iler."

I said "All right" to my sister, but no sooner had she turned her back than I set to devising a scheme whereby I could both rock the cradle and spin my new "peerie" (a top) on the pavement below. I hit on a solution of the problem by tying a long string to the cradle, and, having lead the connection right down the stairs, proceeded to spin my "peerie" on the pavement, and give an occasional tug at the string that was attached to the cradle.

But presently in my enthusiasm for the "peerie" (which was "sleepin' richt bonnie"), I forgot the string in my hand till the shrieks of the infant, on whom the cradle had turned turtle, indicated the price of my absent-mindedness. The next instant my sister appeared at the closemouth, and, having dropped her wash-basket with a thud, delivered me a smarting smack on the side of the face.

Enraged and insulted, I did not wait to pick up the schoolbooks I had deposited at the closemouth. I was off like a wounded deer "hame tae ma mither's." I was simply consumed with rage at the indignity I had suffered and in such a state of mind that I did not take time to consider the distance—18 miles—I had to tramp to reach home.

About five miles out from Aberdeen a kindly-looking woman, whose buirdly form took up almost the whole of her doorway, eyed me rather suspiciously as I approached.

"Faur (where) are ye gaun, my loon?" says she, and I held down my head ever so guiltily.

"Eh?" she rejoined with the air of one having made a good discovery. "I'm thinkin' ye've run awa' frae yer fowks."

I then told her of what had happened and that I was now on my way to my mother at Banchory.

"Banchory!" she exclaimed. "Yer name's Jimmie Skinner, isn't it, an' ye were here a filey since wi' yer brither Sandy playin' th' bass fiddle at a ball, eh? Come awa' intae th' hoose, ma puir loon, an' I'll gie ye a piece."

Sleek or Glaze?

Inside her hospitable home she asked me, "Will ye hae a sleek or a glaze?" and, without awaiting my decision, proceeded to supply me with the latter.

For the benefit of Southern readers I ought to explain the significance of these northern terms. A glaze is the very quintessence of hospitality and a mark of favour where a juvenile is concerned. It consists of spreading butter on a bannock by means of the right thumb, which has been previously dipped in a bowl of water to ensure cleanliness. A sleek implies the spreading of the butter on the bannock with a knife, which is a more economical or "stingy" method.

The bannock of those days was about six inches in diameter and, not only did my hostess spread it with a liberal coating of butter, but "syne she put treacle on the tap o' that, an' sugar abune a'," and I went on my way rejoicing with a satisfied inner man (or boy)!

Having taken about six hours to do the journey home, a "warm" reception awaited me. My mother, instead of giving me the sympathy I had hoped for, applied the "breem cow" once more. Sandy, when he came in, was furious, and proceeded to chastise me further, but, as showing the contrariness of women even in those days, my mother turned on him and pelted him with the "dish clout," then also quite a favourite instrument of correction with mothers.

Two

Dr Mark's Little Men—Early Triumphs

WHILE I WAS LEARNING THE THREE "R's" at Connell's School, Dr Mark's Little Men, the most famous musical combination of its time, arrived in Aberdeen, and, as elsewhere, created quite a furore. My brother Sandy, who was now in Aberdeen teaching dancing, and enjoying the patronage of so distinguished a client as Sir Charles Forbes of Newe, Strathdon, the grandfather of the present Baronet, was naturally much interested in the boys' band, and went to hear its performance, taking me along with him.

After the concert in the Music Hall, which was then known as the County Rooms, in Union Street, Sandy, who must have been studying my face throughout the performance and gauged the ambition that had arisen within me, turned to me and said—"Would you like to go with them, Jimmie?"

"Yes," I replied, my heart throbbing with joyous anticipation.

The result was an adjournment to the "green room" and an interview with the great Doctor, and all the while the conversation proceeded, the "little men" kept hovering around me, some of them having the effrontery to even lift my kilt in order to inspect my legs. To these youthful Sassenachs (there were no Gaels among them then), dressed, as I was, in Highland costume, I was an object of great interest and curiosity, but the interest evoked was akin to that created by a stuffed bird in a museum!

At the request of the Doctor, I played a tune on the fiddle supplied to me, and having finished it, the Doctor addressed me—"Well, Scottie," said he, "would you like to come with us?"

"Yes," I replied, agog at the prospects.

"When?" he asked.

"Tomorrow!" I answered with alacrity.

The following morning in Forsyth's Hotel, Union Street, where the Doctor was staying, the necessary formalities of the indenture were carried through.

That day (it was in 1855) I left Aberdeen with Dr Mark and his forty boys on a six years' apprenticeship. I was as happy as the proverbial sand-boy, and visualised myself as having now firmly planted my feet on the ladder that led to musical success.

An Indulgent Master

With this wonderful combination I visited about six hundred towns and villages in Scotland, England, Ireland, and Wales before I was sixteen years of age. In Dublin I remember hearing a lecture (or reading) by the famous Charles Dickens in the Round Room of the Rotunda.

Along with the boys travelled a tutor named Powell, whose business it was to attend to our education en route and when settled in a town or city. Sums and dictation while the train was speeding along, I well remember, were a difficult proposition. The conditions did not tend to promote either accuracy or beautiful penmanship.

The Doctor was a very able man, and a rabid teetotaller to boot. The boys played nothing but very high-class music, and it will interest those who labour under the belief that I am a strathspey player and nothing else to learn that when I was ten years of age I was playing such difficult compositions as the overtures from *William Tell, Maisonella, Oberon, and Zampa*. Dr Mark's object was to educate orphans of the musical profession, and if they failed to show signs of musical ability by the time they were fourteen years of age, it was then not too late for them to be apprenticed to a trade—an arrangement that prevented their becoming useless members of society.

The Doctor, while a strict disciplinarian, really loved the boys under his charge, and was very indulgent of their foibles. The boys, for instance, used to carry with them from place to place all their pet birds and animals. My pet was a tame starling, which I taught to do a lot of tricks. Other pets included rabbits, white mice, doves, &c., and our arrival in a town very much resembled the advent of a combined aviary and menagerie. Travelling from place to place, we always had a carriage to ourselves, and a pretty big carriage it took to hold us. It was no unusual thing for a number of the company to lose the train, and come on with the next, to receive a keel-hauling from the Doctor.

Going down from Manchester to London, when I was still the "raw" member of the troupe, we played a game which, I believe, is still common among boys—namely, "birds in the bush." One boy holds up his hands, which hide a number of marbles. Another has to guess the number held. If he guesses aright the marbles are his, and so on. Well, the young Scottie, whom they were inclined to treat as a simpleton, "rookit" the lot of them of their marbles, and they resented this very badly. Some of them started to stick pins into my legs and called me "porridge legs." I stood it until I could stand it no longer, then I hit out and gave one of my tormentors a "lovely black eye."

Dr Mark didn't sympathise with my views on the decorative art of the person, and I got a taste of his gutta-percha whip to indicate his disapproval.

Blessing in Disguise

The result was that for a time I felt sore both in body and spirit, but, getting interested in my work, and with the other boys showing more respect, and some of them awe, of Scottie, I soon forgot my troubles and was quite happy.

In everyone's life the element of chance, I believe, plays an important part. Chance, Kismet, or Destiny, or whatever you care to call it, led me into a scrape which, so far from proving a drawback, was the greatest blessing in my musical career. Let me explain.

Dr Mark's "Little Men" had performed on the Saturday night at Luton, and on the Sunday all the boys went out to enjoy themselves. I went with a certain section. We came to a pump, and I held the handle while a few of them put their mouths down for a drink. When it came to my turn, the lad who was holding the handle intentionally turned the pressure on so strongly that the water dashed up the insides of my sleeves, and, without much parley, I lashed into him and gave him a proper dressing-down. Of course, the matter was reported to Dr Mark, who ordered, as punishment, that I be sent back to Manchester, where his headquarters and college were, immediately.

Now, had I remained with the forty boys on tour, I am certain I would never have gained fame as a violinist or become known as the "Strathspey King." Just prior to my return to Manchester, Rougier, a French violinist from the Paris Conservatoire (and a member of Charles Halle's Manchester Band), joined the staff, and I was really in luck's way in finding myself under his tuition. I unhesitatingly ascribe all the success that has been mine to the skilful instruction I received from Rougier. Chance, you see, was an important factor in my career.

As I told you in the previous instalment, my brother taught me to play by ear, and, clever boy that I was, I managed to conceal the fact from Dr Mark, but when I was returned, in disgrace, to the college at Deansgate, Manchester, discovery was imminent in the hands of such an expert and close observer as Rougier.

Right from the start he was suspicious of my method, and I fell into a nice little trap he laid by writing down a different tune from the name given above the score. Rougier, I think, took rather kindly to me, instead of being annoyed at my deception, and right away commenced to teach me the theory of music, and, after several months steady work and skilful tuition, I was passed out to rejoin the "Little Men." My own enthusiasm, fortified now by a knowledge of the rudiments of music, carried me along wonderfully, and even led me into ruses for which, if discovered, I would have, to say the least, been severely reprimanded. One of these was the purchase, in company with a like enthusiast, of 2d. worth of sticks, and 2d. worth of coke, lighting a fire in the cellar below the College, and practising there until two o'clock in the morning!

I was not long on tour with the band again before I contracted smallpox at Hereford. This held me up for six weeks, and the band was in Glasgow when I rejoined it once more.

A Royal Command

We were in Perth station one day when news arrived that Queen Victoria and Prince Albert, her Consort, were shortly to pass through on their way back from Balmoral Castle. As the Royal train steamed slowly into the platform, Dr Mark led his "Little Men" in *God Save the Queen*.

The Prince Consort subsequently stepped out of the Royal saloon, shook hands with the Doctor, and conversed with him in German for several minutes. The boys understood that the Prince was thanking the Doctor and his boys for their reception, and that he had promised to speak to the Queen about us.

The sequel developed six weeks later at York, when Dr Mark and his "Little Men" were ordered by wire to Buckingham Palace for a command performance. Well I remember the excitement caused by the announcement. Even the Doctor himself lost his customary sang froid, and was quite excited at the prospect of playing to Royalty. The first thing he did was to order a complete new outfit for each of the forty boys who were to play, and the result was that, financially, the command performance was a heavy loss to him, but by the added prestige gained he hoped to have made it up before long.

Musically, our appearance before the Queen and her Consort, on 10th. February 1858, could not have been more successful. At the close, Mr S. S. Anderson, Director of Her Majesty's Private Band, eulogised the band in no unstinting fashion, remarking that our execution was perfectly wonderful. The Queen and her Consort, he added, had derived the utmost pleasure from our visit, and wished the band every success.

An experience I had with the band at Bristol is also worth recalling. For the first three years of their apprenticeship the boys received no payment, but for the fourth year they were paid 2s.6d. per week, for the fifth 5s., and for the sixth 7s.6d., but, truth to tell, we hardly ever saw any money, the condition of the Doctor's exchequer being generally pretty low.

At Bristol, several of us found ourselves in such bad financial straits that we decided we must "raise the wind" by some means or other. We had seen numbers of itinerant bands in the streets, and, imagining that they did quite a good thing, we decided to experiment in this direction. Six of us accordingly took our instruments out on to a Bristol street, and were busking (street playing) before a hotel, when the Doctor came upon the scene and put the lid on our little scheme before we had collected many coppers.

A Great Showman

The Doctor, who was a big-hearted man, did not indulge in any reprisals. I believe he knew it was financial trouble, and not a desire for fun or horse-play, that led us to do what we did. As a showman, I believe, he was on a par with the late Willie Frame, the "Man U Know," and would even have given Dr Walford Bodie a hard run for it. One of his favourite practices was to take the entire forty boys on the afternoon before the performance to a baker's shop, from which he would buy forty biscuits. Then he would set the boys off one by one, at an interval of twenty or thirty yards, each with a biscuit in his hand.

People would stop and stare at the long line of biscuit-devouring lads, and naturally ask, "Who are they?" And the answer would be forthcoming, "Oh, Dr Mark's Little Men—they're appearing in————Hall to-night."

I think that I ought to mention here that, although I was the only boy in the band who wore and appeared on the platform in a kilt, I was not the only Scots boy of the company. There were other two—one from Dundee, and the other from Aberdeen. I forget the name of the former, but the latter was

G. S. Mackay, who was in the band during my last three years with it, and was in it when I left. He subsequently became violinist and leader of the orchestra in H. M. Theatre, Aberdeen.

The band was in Glasgow when I "took my hook" with three months of my six years' apprenticeship still to run. The Doctor did not take the trouble to chase me up like a School Board Attendance Officer. On a previous occasion, when I had deserted him on a return visit to Aberdeen, I had stayed overnight with an uncle in the "Granite City," who next morning put me in the train for Tillicoultry, where the "Little Men" were due to appear that night. Possibly Dr Mark thought I should reappear with the same alacrity on this occasion, but I didn't. I hied home to my mother in Aberdeen, whither she had removed from Banchory. The truth is, I was suffering from home-sickness.

Sandy by this time was a soldier, and had taken part in quelling the Indian Mutiny. He rose to the rank of sergeant, and held the distinction of being not only the best shooting sergeant of his regiment (79th Camerons), but also of being the sergeant of the best shooting company of the regiment.

It is not easy to recognise Mr J. Scott Skinner with his "side lappets." He is on the reader's left. With him is his brother Sandy, who gave him his first lessons in violin playing.

Arrived home in Aberdeen, I was soon in touch once more with my old friend, Peter Milne, to whom I confided that I now wanted to train as a teacher of dancing. Peter, ever ready to assist, took me along to the late "Professor" William Scott, of Peterhead, who at that time resided in Stoneywood, Aberdeen, and was employed in the card department of the local mills. Mr Scott was a great scholar, highly cultured, and handsome into the bargain, and had a regal manner and bearing. Thirty years or so later the "Professor" travelled on tour with me as an elocutionist. Alas! old Peter Milne, the "Professor," and his brother "Dauvit" are all gone! I only am left, it would seem!

A One-Sided Bargain

"Professor," said Peter, when the dancing master had agreed to teach me, "Jimmie's like oorsel's, he's no' overburdened wi' bawbees, an' ye'll jist hae tae tak' him as canny as ye can."

"Oh," said the Professor, "I think the best thing we can dae is jist tae tak' him, gie him credit for twinty year, an' meet in heaven an' settle up!"

Thus the bargain, very favourable to me, was sealed, and for two nights a week for nearly a year I trudged out and in the four miles between Stoneywood and my home in order to put me in the way of earning my livelihood as a dancing teacher. The "Professor" taught me the quadrilles, polkas, &c., and many a pleasant night I spent under his hospitable roof. The "Professor's" wife and daughter and I used to go through the quadrilles, and to complete a set had to bring in chairs, which we swung round in approved fashion.

When I had become proficient I sallied forth as a full-blown teacher, carrying my operations away up into the Strathdon region. I gathered together quite a number of classes, for which I acted both as dancing instructor and fiddler. Change is the breath of life, and such was the motive that sent me on perhaps the most adventurous three months of my career. I had gone with Peter Milne to play at a concert at Penicuik, near Edinburgh, and while there heard of an amateur opera troupe in the capital who could be doing with a fiddler, so, leaving Peter, I threw in my lot with this enthusiastic combination, and was then, although I knew it not, on the high road to adventure. There were nine of us in the troupe. They were, as far as I can remember, Brown and Mackay (the promoters), who played the bones and tambourine; T. T. V. Lauric, pianist; Johnnie Wilkie, harmoniumist; Evan Alger, sand dancer; Bill Thomson, baritone; two youths named Reid, who were alto and tenor respectively, and myself.

By some means or other an Irishman from Belfast named Mackenzie (seems a contradiction in terms, doesn't it?), who had a bit of money, was induced to finance the troupe as a professional enterprise under the name of the New Orleans Company. We did a sort of Christie Minstrel show, and I assure you it was quite a smart production. I appeared under the name of Mr Grace Egerton, and a blackened face and a wig effectively concealed my identity from any one of the audience who should happen to know me.

We toured in the South of Scotland and the North of England, and (I believe it was on my advice) tried to storm the dour citadel of Aberdeen. Here I appeared without being recognised, which was perhaps just as well, but after the show I made the acquaintance of the lady who was destined to be my wife.

Back to Aberdeen

Well, to condense the story, in the course of 12 weeks' tour we dropped about £200 in expenses. It was really shameful the way the poor (or, should it be, rich?) fellow was bled. Not only did he lose money on the concerts, but certain members of the troupe sponged on him mercilessly.

When the company burst up at Halifax I trekked back to Aberdeen, and later resumed dancing classes at Alford.

In 1862 I attended two great Highland gatherings in Ireland—one at Belfast and the other at Bray, near Dublin.

The night before the Bray games I felt far from well. An excruciating pain in my side suggested inflammation, and the other performers— athletes, dancers, pipers, &c.—were going to leave me in my bedroom, declaring I was unfit to appear. Leeches had been put to the sore spot the night before, but, despite this fact, I was determined not to miss the games at any cost, so I jumped out of bed and followed the others to the field.

Before the Lord-Lieutenant and 14,000 people I secured several first prizes for dancing. After a great ovation I danced the sword dance, and played my own accompaniment on the fiddle.

I got first prize for the Highland Fling, but I honestly believed it should have gone to John M'Neill, of Edinburgh. I said so to him, and offered him the three guineas prize, but John, in refusing it, said, "Na, na, I winna hae that; ye're the best man that I've seen come out o' the North, an' I'll be pleased tae hae a dram wi' ye."

My Inverness Triumphs

The following year at Inverness, when I was only 19 years of age, I secured my biggest success so far. I had a splendid reception for dancing, but dancing masters were then debarred from taking prizes. However, I had my fiddle with me, and when, the day following the games, a violin competition came off in Farralin Park School I promptly entered. There were eleven entries from all parts, including Dundee, Edinburgh, and Glasgow. Six county gentlemen were the judges—namely, Cluny Macpherson, Roderick Kemp (Talisker), Captain Menzies (Carrbridge), Rev Dr Macgregor, Major Rose, and W. F. Wisdom (secretary).

The railway journey to Inverness from Aberdeen at that time, in length of time taken, was almost equivalent to the ride from Aberdeen to London, owing to a long wait at Keith. On arrival I crossed the street, and found a snug, wee, white-washed and green-thackit hoosie, where I took up my temporary abode with Granny Campbell, on the spot where now stands the Imperial Hotel.

Mr Lowe, dancing master, had the band of the Northern Meeting playing to his children's assembly in the afternoon, and lent his best players for the violin competition; but, in spite of all, I came out first in playing Marshall's *Marquis of Huntly's Farewell*. By request of Cluny Macpherson, I then played *Auld Robin Gray*, and finally conducted the other players (eleven of them) in the roosin' strathspey an' reel *Clach na Cuddin*.

"Gentlemen," said Cluny Macpherson in an eulogistic speech,"we have never before heard the like of this from a beardless boy. This boy will be heard of some day."

I quote this paen of praise in no egotistical vein, for my fundamental belief is that art is not competitive; but I am human enough to hope that I have to some extent fulfilled the prophecy of the famous Cluny. Since 1863 I have, of course, had many successes at similar gatherings, for I never believed in failure after that.

And here, least what I have written should be interpreted as inordinate horn-blowing, let me tell you of a little incident that happened some time later in my career. After a concert in Keith, two youths, with tear-stained faces and a woebegone expression, came to me with a somewhat strange request.

"Oh, Mr Scott Skinner," said the elder of the lads, "oor faither's deein', an' if ye'll come an' play him a bit spring (a tune), he'll pass awa' contentit. He's jist ravin' for ye."

To refuse such pleading was impossible, so I went to the house, and found an octogenarian, wearing a red nightcap, and breathing a fetid atmosphere, lying on a most uncomfortable and dirty bed. I did not, however, let this sordid environment disturb me. Rather it stirred my sympathy for the old man, who, it was plainly to be seen, was getting near the end of his tether, and I determined to put my whole soul into my playing. I played him quite a lot of airs, including the *Marquis of Huntly's Farewell* and *Auld Robin Gray*, and I honestly believe in that death-chamber I played as I have never played before. And when I stopped, a thin, wheezy voice came from the bed -

"Ah, weel, Scott Skinner," it said, "ye're a gey guid fiddler, but ye couldna' play *The Futteruck wi' the Fite Fit!* (*The Ferret with the White Foot!*)." Having delivered this volley, the old man turned his face to the wall, and expired almost immediately.

My own playing, inspired by the thought that I was the witness of the closing of another human profit-and-loss account, had wafted me to ethereal regions, but the cynicism of the old man about to pass into eternity brought me back to the chilly earth (and the stuffy smell of the room) with what is commonly described as a "dull thud!"

Three

When I Was Dancing Master at Balmoral—Willie Blair, the Queen's Fiddler

MY BROTHER SANDY'S RETURN FROM THE ARMY in 1868 found me doing quite well as a teacher of dancing and deportment in the Ballater district. Subsequently I had the honour of teaching Queen Victoria's tenantry at Balmoral, as the direct result of the Queen's intervention on the subject. It happened thuswise—

Her Majesty one day asked Ross, her piper, to play his pipes in the castle grounds, adding that he was to invite the children of her tenantry to be present to enjoy themselves. When the Queen appeared on the scene amazement was written on her face.

"Why are the children not dancing?" she demanded.

"Oh, your Majesty," replied Dr Robertson, her commissioner, "nobody here teaches dancing, and the children cannot dance."

"Is there not a dancing master anywhere in the neighbourhood?" she asked.

"Yes," was the reply, "there's one at Ballater—a young man named Scott Skinner."

"Well," was Her Majesty's command, "give him every encouragement to come here and teach the children to dance. I want to see all the children dancing. I will give the Iron Ballroom for his classes." (The Iron Ballroom was where the ghillies used to dress in the summer time).

Dr Robertson accordingly came to Ballater, and asked me to start dancing classes at Balmoral. I gladly agreed and three times a week I tramped between the two places, a distance of eight miles, in order to give Her Majesty the satisfaction of seeing the children dance. I happily succeeded, and the Queen, I understand, was greatly pleased at the change in the situation, calisthenically speaking.

In all I taught 125 pupils in the Iron Ballroom, and I sometimes wondered where all the loons (boys) and quinies (girls) came from. This was really one of the jolliest periods in my whole career. The tenantry and the officials simply loaded me with kindness. Every night I was there I got a lovely salmon to my tea—not the tinned stuff, but the "rale Mackay" fresh from the river.

I subsequently had the pleasure and honour of an invitation to a large ball given by the Queen at Balmoral. John Brown, the Queen's right hand man, was then in his heyday, and I remember him shoving me right up to where sat Her Majesty in company with the then Duchess of Atholl."Noo, Skinner," he said in quite a loud voice when opposite the Queen (he didn't seem to care whether she heard or not!), "ye're in the richt quarter noo! Shak' yer fit, man! Shak' yer fit!" (foot).

Breezy Willie Blair

Here it would not be unfitting to tell you that at a later period (about 30 years ago) my son Manson had the honour of dancing before Her Majesty. He was about ten years of age at the time. The Queen was quite taken up by the lad's performance, and graciously sent one of her equerries into the ring to ascertain the boy's name.

Spoken to by a haughty official, the lad took fright and started stammering. He had the idea that his name was being taken to the Queen on account of some misdemeanour of which he had been guilty. But when I explained the real significance of the equerry's visit, he was quite pleased and flattered.

Manson, who is now forty years of age, and a married man with a family, resides in Sydney, Australia, whence he returned, like his Uncle Sandy of old in the Indian Mutiny, to serve his King and country in France during the recent war. Prior to that he had done exceedingly well as a dancer in Australia. His success was largely due to the training he received from Madame de Langlee (my brother Sandy's widow), to whom I shall have reason to refer later.

A very original character at Balmoral at this time was Willie Blair, the Queen's fiddler, who lived at Balnacroft, near Balmoral. He was in great demand for balls and jollifications of all kinds around Balmoral. He was very outspoken, and it did not matter to him who was present if he felt he had a grievance. He would air it in spite of anybody and everybody, no matter what their rank or station was. As he was the Queen's favourite musician when residing in her Highland home, he was allowed a certain amount of licence by the officials.

During any festivity if anyone chanced to ask him; "Hoo are ye th' nicht, Wullie?" the answer would come, accompanied by an ingratiating smile; "Aw, I'm sair needin' a rub o' rosit," which was Willie's fly fiddler's way of soliciting a dram.

It is recorded that a certain Duchess, staying with the Queen at Balmoral, made bold to ask if he would play *Patience,* meaning the operatic piece so popular at that time. Willie probably knew nothing of such high-falutin' melodies, and, in addition, his hearing was not of the best, so you can judge the chagrin and surprise of the titled dame when came the retort; "Patience! God a wat, we've ha'en patience—nae the fu' o' yer moo' the nicht!"

Willie had a band to supply occasionally. One night they had gone over the hill, to find on their return that the river was in spate. Nothing daunted, they used the bass fiddle to ford the river one at a time. Whether or not the instrument was of any use afterwards I am unable to say.

Substitute for Snuff

Snuff was a passion with Willie, and the following also illustrates the sense of humour possessed by his spouse.

"Did ye get my snuff frae the village?" Willie asked her one night.

"Naw, naw," she replied, "the grocer was tellin' me that snuff's noo saxpence the 'unce, an' that's ower muckle tae pey for't."

"Whit am I tae dae then?" asked Willie in a petulant voice.

"Och," replied his wife sardonically, "ye can jist kittle (tickle) yer nose wi' a straw!"

Willie lived to a good old age, and many a night his elbow did jink and diddle!

Of another fiddler who lived in the Balmoral district about this time the following story is told. On the way home from a dance, at which he had imbibed not wisely but too well, he got lost, and landed in a pig-sty, and when consciousness was beginning to return to him a big sow was snorting at his ear. Thinking he was still at the dance (or another dance!), the old fiddler irritably exclaimed—"Nane o' yer confounded vampin' here; face the music," and hit the sow a resounding whack on the lug!

The temptation to tell a story about a Balmoral gamekeeper, suggested by a glimpse of a photo of Willie Blair on this page, is too strong to be resisted. "Flapper" bonnets were very common when I was a young man, especially at shootings, when the flaps were pulled down over the ears to shut out the noise of the guns.

Donald M'Tavish wore one of these bonnets day in, day out, but one day his friends were astonished by his appearance with a cap minus the flaps. One of them was bold enough to ask the reason for the sartorial heresy.

"Weel, man," said Donald, "I've stopped wearin' th' flapper sin' my accident."

"Accident!" exclaimed his friend. "I never heard o't. Fit wis't, Donald?"

"Ae day," explained Donald, "I met a gintleman, an' he offered me a dram, an' I didna hear him. Sae I'm takin' nae mair risks!"

About this time the then Sir Charles Ross, of Balnagowan Castle, requested that I should teach him to play the fiddle. Sir Charles was a man of many idiosyncrasies. Thirty cigars a day would be about the average he smoked, or rather wasted. He would only smoke about a couple of inches of each, fling the remainder in the fire, and start on a fresh one. He was lucky that he could afford it!

He was extremely fond of a good story, and I believe it was more my abilities in that direction than my skill as a violinist that prompted him to call on my services. The present Sir Charles was only about five years old at that time, and I had the honour of teaching him the "light fantastic toe." He, of course, is the inventor of the famous Ross rifle.

"I'm tired of fiddling," said the old Baronet to me one day. I had been teaching him by ear, and he had only tackled one tune which, it was very evident, he should never be able to play. "Tell me a story," he requested, laying down his fiddle with an air of boredom.

Moody and Sankey were at this time in Aberdeen, and I thought a yarn concerning one or other of the famous evangelists would be topical, and tickle Sir Charles. So I told him the story of a drunk man rebuked by Moody, and the Baronet was all attention.

This devotee of Bacchus was trying to get home to a place on the Don side. First of all he got into a train for Stonehaven, and was ejected by a ticket-checker; then he tumbled into a train for

Willie Blair, the Queen's fiddler, a "worthy" of his day.

24

Ballater, and again was convinced of his error. Finally he landed in the Peterhead portion of a north-bound train, and found himself in a compartment in which sat Moody and Sankey, bound for a series of meetings at Peterhead.

A Strange Bet

Naturally, in his drunken state, the man made himself a bit of a nuisance. Moody gazed at him, more in pity than in condemnation, and then spoke slowly and deliberately.

"Do you know where you're going to, sir?" he said.

"Na," came the answer.

"Well, you're going to perdition," was the stern rejoinder.

"Eh?" exclaimed the maudlin one, waking up somewhat; "I'm in the wrang train again!"

While I was teaching at Balmoral and Ballater I succeeded in introducing Sandy to Braemar and Gairnside, and in these places he did very well. As a result of my success at Inverness there was now a demand for me at local concerts as a solo player, and I recall some very amusing experiences of such concerts.

At Banff two farmers, who had driven twenty miles to hear me, had an interesting discussion on my abilities. One of them had never previously heard of me, but the other had heard me, and knew all about me, and had been telling his friend what a marvellous player Scott Skinner was. One of my selections was *The Birlin' Reels* (not *Berlin Reels*, as one English newspaper termed them, for there are no German sausages on my kilt!).

Towards the end this composition reaches a tremendous climax, and the two farmers, watching my bow skidding up and down the strings and the pianist's fingers flying helter-skelter over the keys, worked themselves into a frenzy of excitement, till the one who hadn't heard me before, unable to contain himself any longer, jumped up from his seat, and in a raucous voice exclaimed; "I'll bet five bob the quinie (girl) gets there first!"

Caught in a Snowstorm

After I married the lady who, it will be recalled, I first met in Aberdeen when travelling with the short-lived New Orleans Company, I settled down in Aberlour and carried on there and in the immediate neighbourhood for several years as a dancing master.

Before the new line with the loops had been opened from Aberdeen to Banff, the journey between these places was a tedious one indeed. In Banff I had a collection at this time of about 120 pupils, in the teaching of whom I was assisted by Jeanie Meldrum, my adopted daughter. She lived in Banff.

I remember we had left ourselves just little enough time to catch the train at Craigellachie, and we had to dash off without dinner, for which my wife's mother had prepared a chicken. At the last moment, on the suggestion of my mother-in-law, we packed the chicken into a basket and took it with us. My wife and Manson, who would be about two years old, accompanied me on this memorable journey. This happened about forty years ago, but so terrible a journey did it prove that its details remain indelibly imprinted on my memory. It snowed and whistled the entire night, and the train seemed but to crawl along. So intensely cold did it become in the cheerless compartment, with the snell wind whistling through many holes in the floor, that my wife and I, fearing danger to little Manson,

Manson Scott Skinner as a child. He is now in Sydney, and fought with the Anzacs in the war.

wrapped him up in a rug and strapped him to the rack above our heads. There, we considered, he was much warmer than reclining on either of our knees. Of course, the wee chappie was soundly asleep, otherwise such an unorthodox "crib" would not have been acceptable to him.

What I feared practically ever since we had started on the train was fulfilled at Knock Station, where it was found impossible for the train to proceed further, the snow on the line being now four feet deep. The passengers (happily there weren't very many) were ordered out of the train. Where the others spent the night I don't know, but I cannot tell how relieved I felt, considering I had a wife and young infant on my hands, when I found I was intimately acquainted with the stationmaster, a Mr Walker, and heard him offer the hospitality of his home for the night.

Fiddling Away Snow

Next day we got to within a couple of miles or so of Glenbarry, and with my pupils, who were paying me a guinea for twelve lessons, expecting my arrival, and being unable to wire, I naturally felt a bit upset. My wife and I got out and (I was carrying the baby) tried to restore the circulation of our blood by stamping our feet on the snow-covered ground, but as we sank down in it we only added to our discomforts.

Our plight was indeed dire, but when I looked ahead of the engine I saw about 100 navvies making a heroic effort to clear the line for our benefit. Poor devils! They were as cold as an Esquimo's beard, and it occurred to me, being a feeling sort of chap, to help them in some way. The idea of setting to work with a pick or a shovel didn't appeal to me, so I jumped into our compartment, fetched my fiddle out of its case, and commenced playing *The Miller o' Hirn* to them.

The effect was magical. The air is a jaunty and lively one, and to realise my ulterior motives, I played it with an even faster tempo than usual in order to expedite the navvies' labours. The scene would have been comical in the extreme to the passengers if they had been able to view it from a coign of comfort.

As the result of my labours (combined with those of the navvies, of course) I believe the line was cleared at least an hour before it would have been had there been no fiddle on the job!

Some years later I decided to try for "bigger game," speaking in a terpsichorean sense, and, with Elgin as my headquarters, where we lived for about twelve years, I penetrated into all the towns of any size that were accessible. Inverness, Nairn, Elgin, and Forres I tapped successfully, and even further north in Dingwall, Tain, Invergordon, Golspie, and Wick I had a renumerative quota of pupils. My reputation as a teacher of dancing and deportment spread rapidly, and other teachers who were there before me, some of them trading on the label of having taught Royalty, were driven out before it. Practically all the nobility and gentry in the north, who wished to have their children taught the etiquette of the ballroom, were ere long bestowing their patronage upon me.

Among these was Lady Ashburton, of Lochluichart Lodge, Dingwall. The circumstances of my first meeting with her Ladyship are rather interesting. My wife and I were in the Assembly Rooms in Elgin, teaching a class, when a carriage drove up to the door, and a lady, dismounting, remarked to some people in the street; "I hear a fiddle, and I know who is playing—it is Scott Skinner." Her Ladyship had previously heard me play at Strathpeffer.

Carlyle's Compliment

This was the Right Honourable Lady Louisa Ashburton, whose London address was Kent House, Knightsbridge. She was staying for the time being at the Gordon Arms Hotel in Elgin. She came right in and, having introduced herself to my wife and me, asked me; "Will you come to Lochluichart Lodge and give my daughter (the Hon Miss Baring) dancing lessons?"

Of course, I readily consented, and was well paid for my services. The Hon Miss Baring, whom I taught quadrilles, polkas, &c., afterwards married Lord Northampton. She died rather suddenly several years ago, but Lord Northampton, who was a frequent visitor while I was teaching his fiancee, is still alive.

John Ruskin and Thomas Carlyle were frequent visitors to Lochluichart also when I was there. I did actually meet Carlyle, but, as students of his life will know, the author of the "French Revolution" (whose MSS of the second book of that great work, like the documents I had kept for this life of mine, were carelessly burned by someone who didn't know their value) was a taciturn chiel, and was not very communicative when he spoke to me.

It was my custom, after having given the Hon Miss Baring her lesson, to adjourn to the gardener's cottage, and give them a tune or two on my fiddle. On one occasion I played *Tullochgorum*. Carlyle, passing by on one of his solitary walks, stopped to listen, and afterwards remarked to Lady Ashburton; "I heard Scott Skinner ower by playin' *Tullochgorum* rale weel wi' the lang bow," by which he meant the playing of the whole measure with as few sweeps of the bow as possible, probably only four. This compliment was quietly conveyed to me, and I appreciated it very highly from the lips of so distinguished a man and judge as Thomas Carlyle.

My success at this time could hardly have been greater. I had the patronage of all the big private families in Ross-shire, Inverness-shire, Elginshire, and Banffshire. My minimum charge was a guinea per twelve lessons. I was making about £750 a year, and was able to drive to and from the residences of my pupils in my own private trap, drawn by a beautiful pony. This equipment cost me about £150.

Stormy Times

But by and by life's barometer, by reason of internal domestic tragedy, was once more set "stormy" for me. The crash came suddenly, and in a single day I was roofless, wifeless, and penniless. I have no intention of dwelling on those bitter days. Even the memory of them is too bitter for me to stand their recapitulation, and my readers, I am sure, would not enjoy a recital of those tragic events.Suffice it to say that I journeyed to Aberdeen, a sad and broken-hearted fiddler. Despondent, I lay quiescent for a bit, but my innate optimism reasserted itself, and I commenced to re-build the broken structure of my life. Some people may have concluded that I went to a model lodging-house in Aberdeen, but not at all. I had still the germ of pride and self-respect in those troubled days. It was in the Waverley Hotel I found temporary asylum (appropriate word, for I did think I was going mad!), and there I managed to maintain myself by the sale of little printed slips of my own compositions (for I had been composing profusely up till this time) at 6d. a piece. One gentleman, I remember, bought 100 copies from me at "one fell swoop," and I felt the sun had commenced to shine for me once more.

While in Elgin, I might say, I made the acquaintance of the poet "La Teste" (William Leith Hay Tester), who wrote the words for my tune "Glenlivet", one verse of which runs—

> *Scott Skinner's made anither tune,*
> *Th' verra dirl o't reached the moon,*
> *While ilka lassie and her loon*
> *Commenced tae dance sae frisky, oh;*
> *Th' burden o' th' sang was this,*
> *We never felt sic lunar bliss,*
> *Anither reel an' syne a kiss*
> *Ower guid Glenlivet whisky, oh!*

Happily I recovered from the shock and penury that were the aftermath of the Elgin tragedy, and commenced to work out what might be termed my economic salvation once more. I appeared frequently on concert platforms as a solo violinist, and even risked little enterprises of my own by taking concert parties into rural districts in the North. A very successful tour was one I had of the Dee, Don, and Spey, my cast for which was "Professor" Scott (my old dancing master), elocutionist; Manson (my son), dancer; a pianist, and myself.

An Old Man's Resolve

On the way up to Braemar, I remember, we passed two stone-breakers by the wayside. One was quite a youngster, and the other very old and withered-looking. We were seven miles from Braemar, whither we were driving in a dog-cart.

I started to talk to the young man, and thinking to "cast my bread on the waters," i.e., get a cheap advertisement, I grandiloquently bestowed a ticket for the evening's concert on him. Manson, who always took the money at the door, informed me at the close of the concert that an old man wanted to see me, adding—"He's very like the old man we saw breaking stones on the road this afternoon."

I was surprised, for I never dreamt that the old fellow would have considered the concert at all, otherwise I would have given him a gratuitous ticket along with his young workmate. (It dawned on me later that possibly the latter disposed of his ticket to the old fellow for a pint of beer!)

Sure enough, it was the old stonebreaker who wanted to hold counsel with me, and there was something indefinably different about him from his afternoon appearance.

"Did you like the concert?" I asked him, without thinking I was giving him the very opening he desired.

"Aye, aye," said he, "it was fine, man." He proceeded without a break, "I've been terrible bad this filey back wi' an awfy hoast (cough), an' I can hardly licht my pipe thro' the nicht. I was thinkin' aboot daein' awa' wi' masel', but"—(wiping the tears, imaginary or real, from his eyes)—"efter I h'ard you playin' *The Flooers o' the Forest* I took anither tum'le tae masel', an', says I, 'Jock, ye're gane tae leve a filey langer'."

Whether this reference to my execution of *The Flowers o' the Forest* was complimentary or otherwise readers may decide for themselves. Personally, I have never been able to see how a funeral dirge, no matter how artistically played, could cure a man of suicidal intentions. Yet I could not have played very badly. There were no printed programmes in those days, and the would-be suicide recognised the tune!

Four

WHILE, ON THE WHOLE, I did fairly well financially when running my own companies, it is to be admitted that I now and again struck a "snag"—places which turned out financial Saharas—my visits to which left me richer in philosophic thought but much poorer in coin of the realm.

The case of Cullen is typical of these misfortunes. I had boomed my concert there as "the greatest thing that ever happened," but, in spite of all the booming, the people remained unmoved. At least, if they were "moved" it wasn't in the direction of the hall where the concert was held. Only three persons, if I remember correctly, turned up to enjoy the galaxy of talent I had detrained on the place.

When I returned to the hotel (without having given the concert, of course) a bevy of natives gathered round me and expressed their sympathy. "But, Mr Scott Skinner," said one who seemed to have the approval of the bunch, "we dinna think ye spent eneuch on advertisin' yer concert, an' oor advice is for ye tae tak' th' hall again th' morn's nicht, put oot plenty o' bills, an' gie's anither concert."

Foolish man that I was! I had spent a jolly sight more on advertising than I could afford, and here was I listening to advice to increase my advertising account. And the advice, moreover, came from people who hadn't bothered themselves to come to the concert.

I was tempted and fell. In the retrospect, I admit I was stupid, but who isn't wise after the event? I decided to risk another venture in Cullen, and was astir early next morning to ensure that it would be a gigantic success, I personally supervised the distribution of the handbills, and did various other things which, I was certain, would yield the rare refreshing fruit of a packed house.

A Fiasco

I was quite agog with anticipation when I saw the hall door wide open, but, alas! there was no queue waiting. Still, thought I, they've plenty of time, and they'll be coming all right. But when the time for starting the programme arrived—would you believe it?—apart from the artistes and the hall-keeper, there was only one other person in the hall!

As he hadn't come in by the front door and hadn't paid his "tanner," I began to speculate as to his identity. Presently, however, when he saw there was to be no concert, he approached, and I recognised him as my friend the billposter and distributor of the morning. He had come to collect his account!

My first impulse (as no doubt yours in the same circumstances would have been) was to chase the old fellow for his life, but I checked it, and—stood him a drink. And I may have paid the account as well!

A little party that toured the North thirty years ago—Mr Scott Skinner, his son Manson, and (on left) "Professor" Scott, elocutionist and dancing master.

A public performer is generally expected to have a big number of stories dealing with "digs" and landladies. My experiences of these have, on the whole, been fairly pleasant, and only one incident occurs to me at the moment as being worthy of inclusion here. This happened at Lairg prior to a concert.

It was my custom in those days to buy my own food, and hand it to the landlady to cook. On this occasion I bought linked sausages for my tea, and you can imagine my surprise when the landlady, having removed the wrapper, exclaimed—"Fit's they, Mister Skinner? I niver saw the like afore!"

"They're linked sausages," I explained obligingly.

"And fit wey wid ye cook them?" she asked.

"Oh, jist the same wey as ye'd cook fish," I answered somewhat curtly.

When tea-time arrived I took my place at the table in the "pawlor," and awaited the entry of the foodstuffs. Presently I heard strange sounds coming from the region of the kitchen, and shortly afterwards the landlady, carrying a plate, holding something dimly reminiscent of a haggis, blew into the room, and, placing the dish before me, remarked with a broad smile— "There's nae muckle left o' they things when ye tak' the insides oot o' them, Mr Skinner."

She had done as I advised—cooked the sausages as she would fish, but it was unfortunate for my appetite that the particular fish in her mind's eye at the time of the operation should have happened to be fresh herring.

A Curiosity

It is always interesting (even if occasionally somewhat annoying) to see yourself as others see you. After a concert given by a company of mine at Keith, I was just leaving the hall, which was then in darkness, when I heard my name mentioned in a conversation proceeding between two old women a few yards from the hall door. I hung back and listened.

"Faur (where) ha'e ye been the nicht, Kirsty?" asked the one of the other.

"Oh, I was in hearin' that great fiddler, 'Leezbith."

"Fit's his name?"

"Scott Skinner."

"Wis he here?"

"Aye."

"Fit a peety. I wid hae lik't tae hae seen him. I've never clappit een on 'im. Fit like is be, Kirsty?"

"Weel, he's like—och, I couldna tell fit like he is, 'Leezbith. Naebody could tell ye that."

"Fit wey, Kirsty?"

"Ye maun just see him for yersel'," declared Kirsty, "for Scott Skinner's jist ane o' th' Almichty's curiosities."

Some of you may be surprised to learn that I regard this description as one of the finest compliments ever paid to me. What the old woman meant to imply was that I was so steeped in character as to be indefinable. My humble hope is that my personality merits the encomium.

As I am following no particular chronological scheme at the moment, it would be permissible to relate here how I saved a life. It is a pathetic story, so prepare your hankies!

The scene is Union Street Bridge, Aberdeen.

"The Strathspey King," deep in thought (probably composing a new strathspey), walks leisurely east.

Westwards ambles a piece of life's driftwood. (Never mind the point about the impossibility of driftwood walking. I mean a beggar, and as he had a wooden leg, the metaphor isn't so bad!)

Beggar salutes "The King."

"Can you spare a copper?" he asks, in the ingratiating tones and common parlance of his tribe.

"The King," his heart touched, hurriedly searches his pockets, finds a pound note, but nothing smaller, and speaks.

"What would you do if I gave you a pound note?"

"Eh?" gasps the astounded mendicant.

"What would you do if I gave you a pound note?" repeats "The King."

"Man," says the beggar, "I'd drap doon deid."

So "The King," being a kind-hearted fellow and a regular, though anonymous, subscriber to the funds of the R.S.P.C.A., keeps the pound note where it is and—moves on.

Storm-Stayed

It would be about this time that I first made the acquaintance of Miss Jessie Maclachlan, the great Scottish prima donna, and I should like to tell you (excuse the Irishism) of the engagement we didn't fulfil together.

For a special concert under the auspices of the Peterhead Choral Union the following party had been engaged: Jessie Maclachlan, soprano;

Bob Buchanan (her husband), pianist; Stewart Moncur, tenor; and myself.

A snow storm was raging when we left Aberdeen, and when we got to Dyce I expressed the opinion to Bob Buchanan that we would never reach Peterhead that night.

"Nonsense!" was the general chorus of the compartment, "what makes you say that?"

For answer I pointed to the clouds, and added that now popular Asquithian term—"Wait and see."

I was by no means jubilant to find my prophecy fulfilled (I would have felt happier to have gone on to Peterhead and earned my fee for appearing), but fulfilled it was at Mintlaw, where we were informed that the depth of snow on the rails prevented the train from proceeding further.

The party adjourned to Mr Hendry's hotel, which was quite convenient to the station. Mintlaw is only a matter of eight miles from Peterhead, and we thought Mr Hendry would be able to furnish a conveyance for the completion of our journey. But we were mistaken. "Na, na," declared Mr Hendry when we had made the suggestion. "I widna put oot th' worst pair o' horses I hiv in th' stable for a hunner poun' on sich a nicht," and no amount of pleading would induce him to alter his decision.

The result was that we failed through no fault of our own to fulfil our engagement at Peterhead, and after spending a day and a half, storm-stayed in Hendry's Hotel, we returned to Aberdeen.

Inexperienced as I was, I concluded that the Railway Company would be liable to pay compensation to the party, but a young lawyer whom I consulted on the subject dissuaded me from making such an application. "If you're a wise man," said he, "you'll not seek compensation, for if you look at the Company's bye-laws you'll find they do not hold themselves responsible for acts of Providence. A snow storm comes within that category, and you wouldn't get a penny."

So, although I had lost a lot of money, I had to hold my peace.

On this subject of delays in travelling, I am reminded of a case where a too speedy journey was regarded as a grievance. In my boyhood's days, when one could only journey from Deeside to Aberdeen by stagecoach, a chronic complaint of travellers was that the coach never stayed long enough at an inn to allow

Miss Jessie Maclachlan, the famous Scottish prima-donna, who often appeared with Scott Skinner

them to get a decent meal, and many were the ruses employed to delay the coach and ensure a satisfying repast.

On one occasion when a halt had been made at an inn, a number of "Mine Hostess's" silver spoons were suddenly found to have vanished, and the good lady absolutely refused to allow the coach to budge until they were found or restored. This contretemps delayed the coach for what was then thought to be an unconscionable period, but presently two men, who had been enjoying a hearty meal, emerged and explained the situation.

"Here's yer money," said one of them, addressing the landlady, "an' gin ye look yer teapot, wifie, ye'll get yer spunes a' richt," and the stage coach was allowed to depart in peace.

Wanted by Police

Like, I suppose, many other artistes I have frequently been troubled with parasites who fastened on to me at all sorts of inconvenient times. I recall how on one occasion I was rushing to catch a train from Aberdeen to Edinburgh, when one of this troublesome fraternity, all too evidently bent on largesse, collared me—literally. To add to the annoyance of the situation the man was under the influence of liquor, and the spectacle of Scott Skinner, in Union Street, with a drunk man's arm round his neck was galling in the extreme to me. I was carrying my fiddle and my wallet of music, and I had no hopes of disengaging him. He started to ask me a lot of inane questions, which were bound to lead up to a request for money, so I thought of a plan for getting rid of him.

"Let me go man, let me go," I appealed, simulating intense excitement.

"Whit's wrang?" said the man, seeing the look of tragedy on my face.

"I'm in great trouble," I lisped tremulously.

"Whit's gane wrang?" he asked sympathetically.

"Oh, I'm wanted by the Edinburgh police—let me go man."

And, aghast at the thought of "The Strathspey King" requiring to flee before the forces of justice, the maudlin one released his uncomfortable grip, and I dashed off to catch my train, and play at the annual concert of the Edinburgh police.

One of the most novel appearances I ever made was at a private show which I gave to satisfy the whim of a millionaire. Perhaps I do him an injustice in saying that, for he was genuinely fond of music, and Scottish music in particular.

His name was Jake Allan, a North of Scotland man, who had returned home after having made his pile in New Zealand. The fact that he had a million to his name didn't inspire the folks who knew him as a loon to prefix it with "Mr" or suffix it with "Esq"; to them he was just Jake Allan.

When I was living at Monikie, near Dundee, a wire arrived from Jake Allan requesting me to come north to the Strathbogie Arms Hotel, Gartly, near Huntly, to play a strathspey or two for him, as a great favour.

I thought the thing a hoax, and expressed my doubts in an answering wire, but back came another telegram to say that the request was genuine, and would I come at once? So off I went.

In the room were Jake Allan, Joe Dunbar, Huntly, who acted as pianist, and myself. No other person was allowed to enter, but I had not been playing long before a crowd collected outside the hotel, and supplied unsolicited applause at the end of each of my solos.

I played a lot of my best numbers to him, and the millionaire was absolutely delighted. So much so that he gave me seven guineas for my services, paid my hotel expenses, and bought a quantity of my own compositions. So it wasn't a bad "spec" for me.

Jake entertained us right royally, and I remember, when playing *The Valley of Silence*, my tongue's movements were not quite in keeping with the theme, and Joe Dunbar administered me a well-merited rebuke—"Ye're playin' *The Valley of Silence*, 'King', but ye widna think ye were there jist noo."

Jake Allan was then about 70 years of age, but he returned to New Zealand and died there.

A Crooked Compliment

Great friends of mine were the Beatties of Wardhead Farm, Kennethmount. There were two brothers, Charlie and Willie, the former being the painter of the famous picture, "The Laird o' Logie" (William Barclay, Esq, of Logiemuir, near Inverurie).

Charlie was in the habit of going out from Aberdeen and spending the week-ends with Willie, who was the farmer. Both were passionately fond of the fiddle, and both played well, but Willie was easily the better player.

I had frequently been in the vicinity playing at concerts and teaching dancing, and Willie had always invited me up to the farm and got a few "tips" from me on how to play strathspeys. I was their guest one week end when Charlie arrived from Aberdeen, and after tea, the fiddles were produced. Willie led off with *Glenlivet*, and for once in a while Charlie, who was a great wag and "aff-takin' customer," deigned to compliment his brother. "That's weel done, Wullie," he said.

"D'ye think sae?" meekly asked Wille.

"Oh, aye," remarked Charlie, "I suppose ye've been gettin' tips frae Scott Skinner."

"Oh, aye," agreed Willie, who lost his head in face of all the flattery, and proceeded to "put his foot in it." "Charlie," he exclaimed, "d'ye ken whit Scott Skinner says aboot your playin'?"

"Naw," said Charlie, expecting a compliment.

"Lord, man, he says ye canna play ava!"

"Gosh!" replied Charlie, quite coolly, "that's rale funny, for he jist telt me th' same thing aboot you."

So' to use a phrase common in the North, Willie had been "fleein' up tae th' moon tae land in th' midden."

After playing at a ball in Buckie many years ago, along with the Sutherland Brothers, of Elgin, a halt was made at Fochabers on the homeward journey to feed and water the horses, while the musicians took a short walk to stretch their legs. A Highland collie, unnoticed, entered the vehicle during their absence and attacked the parcel of music lying on the seat.

I had recently composed a pretty set of Lancers in Highland airs, the band parts for which were in the parcel, and on being told what had happened, I am reported to have said, "If it's a Hielan' collie, ye canna blame it for wantin' a look at *The Clansmen's Lancers*."

The Musical Dog

This incident reminds me of another concerning a huge St Bernard dog which belonged to the late Mr William Lindsay, of Banchory. My brother Sandy, with his wife, Madame de Langlee, was in Banchory at the time. Mr Lindsay, passing their lodgings one day with the dog, as always for a companion, met Sandy at the door, and was invited in to hear a strathspey. Mr Lindsay eagerly accepted, for he was a strathspey enthusiast.

Before giving the promised strathspey, Sandy played a German valse, which was brought to an abrupt conclusion by the howling of the St Bernard dog.

"Wait a minute," said Sandy, and proceeded to play *Moneymusk*, hearing which the sagacious animal put out his tongue and wagged his tail in ardent appreciation. What a handy dog to have about when an itinerant German band arrives at your door! But that won't be for a long bit, yet I'm thinking.

I believe in an earlier instalment I promised to tell you more about

Madame de Langlee. Her meeting with my brother was quite romantic. Her full name was Madame Finart de Langlee, and she was the daughter of General de Langlee, of the French Army, whose Legion of Honour, bequeathed to her by him, she proudly wore on her breast. For many years, it is also interesting to note, she unsuccessfully tried to establish a claim to the famous Jennings property which was held in Chancery.

Madame de Langlee, Sandy Skinner's wife, who after her husband's death, assisted Mr Scott Skinner as a dancing teacher for many years.

Sandy was on a visit to Nottingham, when, in the hotel at which he was staying, he noticed a card hanging up advertising the fact that Madame de Langlee was prepared to accept pupils for dancing and deportment. Sandy, inspired only with business motives at the time, wrote to Madame. A meeting was arranged, and it was a case of love at first sight. But Madame was as good a business hand as her husband, for, after their marriage, she confessed that prior to fixing the appointment, she had written to the Association of Dancing Masters to ascertain whether or not his letter was bona-fide.

Thereafter they conducted highly successful classes over a wide field, embracing Nottingham, Belfast, Dublin, &c. It was on the death of Sandy that I wired Madame to join me, and together we taught classes in the North for some 14 years. She was an accomplished woman; with great success she taught such graceful dances as the Minuet de la Coeur, and one of her hobbies was the decoration of mirrors with leather flowers, at which she was an adept. She was, moreover, a mother to my motherless boy, and much of his success was due to her expert coaching. It is a matter of great regret to me, however, that Manson could never be induced to apply himself to the violin. It would have been pleasing to me to know that my mantle was to fall on him. While in Elgin, I might have added, Madame de Langlee taught dancing to a number of boys and girls who appeared there in a kinderspiel written and composed by the late Sheriff Rampini.

My brother Sandy's end was, I might have said, very painful and distressing, but even in his last moments his inborn sense of humour did not desert him. As a last possible means of saving his life an operation was decided on. Sandy was informed.

"Ye'd better sen' for a meenister," he remarked to the relatives round his bed.

"A meenister! It's a doctor ye need, Sandy."

"Mebbe," said Sandy, "but if I'm tae be opened, I'm gaein' tae be opened wi' prayer."

Such was the man, witty and whimsical to the last—a man "wha had misfortune great an' sma', but aye a he'rt abune them a'."

Five

The Pathetic Story of Our American Tour—Penniless and Stranded

EVER SINCE MY TRIUMPH AT INVERNESS I had been a fairly regular attender at all the big Highland Gatherings, and, as a result, made many friends amongst the athletes, pipers, fiddlers, dancers, &c.,who appeared. Donald Dinnie I met pretty frequently, and here I should interject that never once did I see Donald the worse of liquor. I saw him quaff unconscionable quantities of milk, but many of the stories circulated as to his capacity for alcoholic refreshment, I am convinced, had no foundation in fact.

Among the many staunch friends I made at those games was piper Willie MacLennan, of Edinburgh, who was also a fine dancer. Willie was one of the most popular figures at these meetings. So great was his popularity that he was simply inundated with requests to tour the United States, and Canada in particular, with a party of his own, and in 1893 he at last decided to take the risk. He was assured that there was no risk in it, but alas as events proved, the risk involved Willie's very life.

It was at Highland Games under the auspices of the Aberdeen Athletic Association that Willie said to me—"Would you care to come to America with me for a three-months' tour?" I said, "Delighted!" and terms, &c., were arranged on the spot.

We left Glasgow in *The City of Rome* (which was then the largest vessel afloat) full of buoyant hope and glorious expectation, and arrived in New York after a pleasant and uneventful voyage.

My first experience of a Yankee hotel was made memorable by the temporary loss of a pair of boots. Before retiring for the night, I placed these outside my bedroom door, expecting, as in a hotel at home, that they would be back there in the morning in a brightly-polished condition.

When I opened my bedroom door the following morning the boots weren't to be seen, and I rang the bell to expedite their delivery. A nigger appeared, and I demanded, "Where's my boots?"

"De boots, sah!"

"Yes," I explained incisively, "the boots I left outside this door last night."

Missing Boots

The nigger was puzzled, but went off to make enquiries. Presently he returned, a smile suffusing his ebony countenance.

"You no' want the boots no more, sah," he explained; "de boss, he give de boots to de poor man."

"But I do want the boots," I shouted, becoming exasperated; "they're a new pair; they're not old boots."

I had about half an hour to wait before the boots were forthcoming, and it seemed that the nigger's explanation was perfectly correct. The practice in American hotels is for the guest to put his boots on as he took them off the previous night, and have them polished up on his feet by a shoe-black on the ground floor. When my boots were found outside my bedroom door, it was concluded that I had no further use for them, and they were accordingly handed over to some poor nigger in need of footwear. And they had the deil's own job finding the needy nigger when I made the rumpus and demanded their return. You may rest assured I didn't make any more mistakes of this kind in Yankee hotels.

The party consisted of Willie MacLennan, piper and dancer; Mabel Munro, mezzo-soprano; Nellie Asher, soprano; Alice M'Farlane, contralto; Dove Paterson, elocutionist; Hector M'Bride, tenor; W.Kinnieburgh, baritone; Jamie Blaikie, pianist; and myself. Of the entire company, Willie MacLennan was the only member who had previously been in either Canada or the United States. This was, in fact, his tenth, and, as it eventuated, his very last voyage.

On the way across—as a matter of fact, when we had been only a few hours aboard—I overheard a lady member of the company remark to another of the ladies, "Say, what's the old bloke going to do?"

"Don't know," was the reply, "but seems funny taking an old chap like that so far away from home, doesn't it?"

That I was offended at this discussion of me is putting it mildly. Truth to tell, I was in a rage, and determined to be even with the fair detractors at the very first opportunity. Of course, my rage was subsequently cooled by the Atlantic breezes, but when I landed on the other side I was still harbouring a desire to show the two ladies in question why I had been included in the party.

Our opening concert in the Lennox Lyceum, New York, right away provided me with the opportunity I ardently desired. I don't believe I ever got a better reception in my life than I got that night, for the audience, one could feel, was liberally spiced with, if not mainly composed of, Scots. At all events, they

A picture of Manson Scott Skinner, taken while he was serving in the Anzacs during the war.

simply went mad over my strathspeys. I was recalled again and again, and when I made my final acknowledgements I stepped into the wings and found together the two ladies who had discussed me at the outset of the voyage.

"Pardon me, ladies," I remarked, with a touch of acerbity in my voice, but with ever so gallant a bow, "that's what the old bloke can do!"

The fair ones were too abashed to make reply, but in time I became quite good friends with both of them, and the two incidents were completely forgotten.

No Make-up

I am always pleased to aver that I belong to the "old school" of artistes. I am a progressive so far as my art is concerned, but a conservative so far as my own face is concerned. That is to say, I never "make-up" for the platform. I never at any time relied on grease-paint and powder to gain effects. I never wanted the audience to concentrate their gaze on my physiognomy; I desired them to concentrate their souls on my music.

I appeared, as usual, without "make-up" in New York, but not long afterwards my stubborness on this score led to a little contretemps.

The manager for a Yankee gentleman who had booked us for a concert in Philadelphia came into the "green room" as the time for starting the programme grew near.

He had not been long in when, facing me, he exclaimed, so that all could hear him, "Say, boss, what's the matter with your face?"

"My face!" I replied, "do you see anything wrong with it? Maybe I haven't so big a jaw as you!" I was pretty angry.

"Steady, old son," said he in mollifying tones, "your nat'ral face is all right, but what about the 'doings', the 'make-up', you know?"

"Not having any," said I.

"Ye don't mean to tell me you are going on with that face," he exclaimed, amazed.

"Ay, and no other," said I.

Dashing to the other end of the room, he lifted a 'phone receiver, asked for a number, and spoke—"Say, guv'nor," said he, "there's an old guy here as won't 'make-up' before he goes on. What am I to do abaht it?"

The reply was evidently to the effect that he was to insist on my "making-up," for he renewed his efforts in that direction. I was obdurate, however, and in the end he had to let me appear with my face as nature made it, subject, of course, to time's amendments.

As I expected, the lack of paint made absolutely no difference to my reception, which was again cordial in the extreme, and the paint-passion manager was amongst the first to congratulate me, adding the ambiguous remark, "Wall, old son, your face is not your fortune."

"No," said I, to clear up the mystery if there was any, "it's my fiddle!"

Apart from the time of my youthful exploits with the New Orleans Company, there is only one occasion when I "made-up." This was at Dundee, and the experiment was made for a joke more that anything else. As a matter of fact, it was so much of a joke that I washed the whole thing off before I went to the platform.

Willie MacLennan's tour, which was to last for three months, but only extended to eight weeks, was a complete financial failure. While we did well in some places, we lost very heavily in many others. The tour was badly managed. In the places where we lost money this was invariably due to the fact that our concert clashed with some important local function or celebration. The centenary of Columbus was one of the "anags" we found ourselves up against.

That the financial embarrassments of the tour were directly responsible for poor Willie MacLennan's death I am not prepared to say, but this much I will say—they certainly hastened it. I shall never forget the last concert at which Willie appeared.

Willie's Last Fling

This was at a town called Pawtuckett. Willie danced the Highland Fling. I was standing in the wings, and right from the commencement of the dance I noticed he was unsteady in his movements, and as the dance proceeded he was simply wobbling from side to side.

"Come here," I shouted to Dove Paterson. "Look at Willie. There'll be nae mair o't efter the nicht," and hardly were the words out of my mouth than Willie came down with a sickening clatter, the back of his head striking the floor.

This happened quite early in the programme. Our first impulse was to drop the curtain and declare the performance at a close on account of the illness of our chief. But during a hurried consultation in the wings it was mentioned that an American audience might resent this procedure, so it was decided to carry on till the finish, giving as few encores as possible. The artistes, if not the audience, were under a cloud for the remainder of the evening, and it was a relief to all of us when the proceedings were over.

Willie's trouble was meningitis. Even before this heart-breaking denouement on the stage we had all noticed that his memory was going, but we little dreamt that he was to die so far away from the "bonnie Scotland" he loved so dearly, and whose music and dances were as the very breath of life to him.

Willie, after attention from a doctor, recovered sufficiently to entrain with us for Montreal, but it was only a temporary recovery, for before Montreal was reached he was again seriously ill. The ladies of the party were prostrated with grief at this sad turn of events, and even the male members were deeply moved. A wire was despatched to relatives of Willie who resided at Montreal, and a few of these were waiting to take him to their home. There, a few days later, one of the best pipers and dancers that ever graced Scotland breathed his last.

Willie's last words to his company were to carry on as best we could until he recovered, for he did not think he was nearing the end, so we telegraphed to Toronto for a dancer named Johnston to take our leader's place, and continued to tour until we returned to Montreal, where we had been booked for a concert. The impression of that night, so full of pathos and tragedy, I shall never forget. Even to write it, although it is 30 years ago, brings tears to my eyes.

Just before the concert began I noticed a man dressed in a kilt and plaid, carrying a case of bagpipes, in the room. He had his back to me, and I did not, therefore, immediately recognise him, but when he turned I saw none other than Willie MacLennan's great rival in piping and dancing, Angus MacCrae, of Callander. In the old country Willie and Angus, in a good sporting sense, had been the greatest of enemies, and many a hefty fight for the honours of the day they had at various Highland gatherings. I was somewhat surprised at Angus's presence, and indicated this feeling in my salutation—"Hullo, Angus, whit's brocht you here?"

"Man," said he, "I'm a valet wi' a gentleman that's steyin' here the noo, an' I jist thocht I'd come alang an' play *The Pibroch* for Willie." This from a man who had been the dead man's most formidable rival I regarded as very honourable and touching indeed.

A Touching Scene

The news of Willie MacLennan's tragic death had got abroad, and the concert in Montreal was regarded as a sort of tribute to the famous piper and dancer. The result was that the house was packed from floor to ceiling, and many, I believe, had to be denied admission. Every Scot and every one of Scottish extraction in the place seemed to have turned out to honour their countryman who had died in exile.

The proceedings opened with *The Pibroch*, by Angus MacCrae, and as the big, strapping piper, his every button covered with crape, moved silently to the platform, you could have heard the dropping of the proverbial pin.

Then Angus, having filled his bag, marched slowly from end to end of the stage, expressing the wild melancholy message of *The Pibroch*, I believe, as he never did before. His whole soul was put into his pipes. He was playing a lament to a man who, despite superficial whims and jealousies, he loved dearly and fervently.

The scene in the auditorium is ineffaceable. I can never forget it. There was not a dry eye in the building, and ever and anon the sound of a frame-convulsing sob would percolate to the wings, where all the artistes, with bowed heads, quivering lips, and tear-stained faces, also paid tribute to their departed chief.

At a later stage I took the platform and played *The Flowers of the Forest*, and as I played with my whole soul a thousand white objects obtruded before me. They were handkerchiefs—the audience were still wiping bitter tears from their eyes.

Mr Scott Skinner in full travelling kit on tour.

I need not dwell further on the events of this memorable concert. It was touching, yea, heartbreaking in the extreme. I might mention, however, that later on Willie MacLennan's body was exhumed and brought home to Edinburgh, and reinterred there in almost equally impressive circumstances. I should have dearly loved to be present, but illness prevented me.

Well, this tour came to an end not long after this. The four vocalists wanted to keep the company together, and offered to tide us over by singing sacred music in churches on Sundays, but the rest of us had too much Scottish grit and independence to listen to such a proposal. Dove Paterson, Willie Kinniburgh, and I, therefore, decided that the best thing we could do was to get home, but as we were almost penniless that, in itself, was a problem.

We were at Scranton at this time. I had a valuable gold watch, and, with the view to "raising the wind," I called in a pawnbroker to put a price on it. "£3.10s," said he, but even if I had starved to death and was never to see my native land again, I should never have let the watch go at that figure. I have a decided objection to being "done," and that would have been the position had I let the watch go at that money. The Jew was out to exploit my penury to the utmost, but I sorted him.

A Pathetic Photo

As showing that even in our great distress we were quite buoyant, I'll tell you of an incident that happened at Niagara Falls while we were down on our luck. I was ever a lover of puns and repartee, whether as a maker or listener, and I remember that at the Falls there was a little steamer anchored. I saw it in the forenoon before any of the others, and had noted its name. Dove Paterson, Willie Kinniburgh, and I, in the absence of a better pastime, due to lack of funds, went down to the Falls in the afternoon, by which time the atmosphere was thickly charged with mist, which lay close down on the water.

Pointing to the little steamer, Dove, who wasn't sure what the object was owing to the mist, asked—"What's that made of?" And, having decided in his own mind that it was a boat of some description, added—"I suppose its made of wood or iron."

The temptation to pun overwhelmed me, and in grandoise fashion I made reply—"No, Dove, it's *Maid of the Mist.*" That, indeed, was the name of the little vessel.

Subsequently Paterson, Kinniburgh, and I struggled to New York. From doing the "la-de-da" in hotels we drifted into lodgings of the meanest description. One day we decided we could remain quiescent no longer. Things were getting so serious that we decided we must map out some plan of campaign, the first objective, if not the only objective, of which was the transport of our now ill-clad "carcases" to Scotland.

Then it was that we remembered two leal countrymen, J. D. Law (a native of Deeside), in Philadelphia, and William Collins, whose home was in Scranton, where we had been shortly before.

The little plan we eventually hit upon was to spend a few of our fast diminishing "bobs" on a group photo of the tried and (t)rusty trio. I wish I had a copy of that card for reproduction here. It would convey a much better idea of our plight and the message it carried to Law and Collins than any words of mine. This picture did indeed tell a story. "Down and out" was written all over it, and its title might well have been "The Three Vagabonds."

The effect was magical, or, shall I say, natural, in the circumstances. Both friends wired and asked if there had been a disaster, and we replied that it was even worse than that. Both of them then repaired to New York with all possible speed, and when I tell you that Collins covered 250 miles to come to our succour you will see that Scottish "clannishness" is no empty figure of speech. In this case it represented also a considerable figure of money.

Neither of them, while sensing that we were in straits, had brought sufficient money to pay three passages home, but with these gentlemen, both in a good business way and of sound credentials, as guarantors, we had little difficulty in booking berths on the homegoing Ancona. And as the parson would say—Thus endeth the reading of the American tragedy. Let not its lessons be lost on you. As for me, its lessons were never lost.

Six

Memories of Dancing Days—The Humours of Touring—Unlucky Thirteen

WHEN I RETURNED FROM AMERICA I made up my mind on two points. Firstly, I decided to have done with dancing. As a solo violinist I meant to stand or fall. Secondly, I decided to make the kilt my platform dress. In America I wore evening dress while performing, and before crossing the "herring pond" my use of the kilt had not been regular.

With the exception of myself, there was no Scottish violinist of any eminence at this time. Mackenzie Murdoch, of whom I hold the highest opinion, was still but a stripling, and the field was held by English fiddlers of the calibre of William Henley and Johannes Wolf, so I felt the time had arrived for me to make a bold bid for national laurels. Success happily crowned my endeavours, and, with its realisation, I bitterly regretted the many years I had wasted as a country dancing master. I was really starting my life's work, as it were, when I was, practically speaking, an old man, and when many others would have been thinking of retiring. However, I put "a stout he'rt tae a stey brae," and conquered.

Apropos my resolution to wear nothing but Highland costume on the platform, I had not been long back from America when I was asked to wire my terms for a concert at Forres, and this was the message I dispatched— "Ten guineas in kilt, seven guineas without." Back came the reply— "Accepted," but it wasn't until I actually arrived in Forres that I learned of the strange interpretation they had made of my telegram, the Secretary informing me that they had conceded the ten guineas to ensure that I did not appear naked!

One winter night when the ground was covered with snow, I was on my way to an engagement in Aberdeen. To keep my feet dry I was wearing snow shoes, which, of course, do not blend very well with the garb of old Gaul.

A Caustic Comment

One of the two women I passed on my way along Union Street was quick to notice the sartorial anachronism, and made me rather uncomfortable by the exclamation to her companion, meant, of course, for me to hear—"Goodness, Meg! Look at it—A Hielan' man wi' snaw-buits."

Which story reminds me of a similar incident which happened at Campbeltown some time later when I was travelling with the company of the late Davie Thomson (of the Aberdeen Beach Pavilion).

This was winter time also, and on the way to the hall I wore the same pair of snow-shoes. These I absent-mindedly forgot to remove when I entered the artistes' room, and actually walked on to the platform wearing them. I must have presented a somewhat incongruous appearance.

Later on I did conclude there was a strange note in the reception given me by the audience as I appeared on the platform, but I did not detect it at the time, and had lifted my fiddle to start playing when I heard a voice in a stage whisper, from the wings say—"Skinner, your snow-shoes."

To have walked off the stage and removed the shoes, I think now, would have been the wiser plan, but, acting on the impulse of the moment, I laid my fiddle on the piano, bent down, slipped off the snow-shoes, placed them below the piano, straightened my back, lifted my fiddle again, and started to play. Of course, these operations did not take quite so long to execute as their description may indicate, but they took long enough in all conscience.

Luckily the audience took my lapse of memory quite good-humouredly, and their unstinting applause at the end of my efforts showed they were in no way annoyed or amused (the latter being a serious thing for a straight artiste) by my unconventional conduct on the platform.

A Quaint Character

But, before dismissing the recollections of my dancing days, I should like to relate a few stories of characters I met in the North of Scotland.

Among these was the late Pipe Major Donald Macpherson, of

Mr Scott Skinner and Miss Jeannie Hendry in sword dance.

Dingwall, who was a fine pibroch player and won a gold medal over the head of such a great exponent as Duncan Campbell. He piped *Duntroon* faultlessly.

Donald joined my evening dancing classes in Dingwall, but because of his age and his eccentric and erratic habits, due to sunstroke, he wasn't popular with the "fair sex" as a partner. He was, however, a well-read and intelligent man, though agnostic to the core. He was a perfect artiste, and he used to play for a couple of hours to get his reeds, &c., into trim.

From him I learnt the various pipe effects, first on the chanter and then on the pipes. Of course, I merely listened, and then tried to produce the same effects on the violin from the meagre pipe scale of nine notes. The fact that pipers can only play on nine notes prompts me to interject the debate between an old fiddler and an old piper.

51

"Get awa' wi' yer pipes," said the fiddler, "ye canna play half-notes."

"Ach," replied the piper, "she would be ashamed tae play less than whole notes."

One day Donald Macpherson, walking through Dingwall, beheld a fine "lum" hat in a clothier's window, which caused him to reflect that he was never bidden to any funerals. Determined to discover the reason, he went in and bought the hat. In less than a month, he received no fewer than seven invitations to funerals!

Some thirty years ago I played at a flower show in Huntly, at which I met Mr Frank Gilruth, the writing master of Dumfries Academy. He belonged to Gartly, and was very fond of strathspeys. I promised to write to him, and we were fast friends before he took his departure.

"Well," said he, "I'll gi'e ye my full address."

"Yes," said I, "but say it slowly an' I'll remember it."

He did so, and I remarked; "Yes, I'll min' something about a fish (gil) and a book in th' Bible (Ruth)."

This idea fairly tickled him, and for quite a long time I began my letters to him: "Dear Fish Bible," and he in turn concluded his: "Yours truly, Fish Bible."

A Queer Address

Madame de Langlee thought of starting dancing classes in Dumfries, and decided to write to my correspondent on the matter. She hunted through my papers for the address, but I didn't know this until the letter was returned because no such person as she had addressed was known, for she had written on the envelope: "Mr Fish Bible, Schoolmaster, Dumfries!"

My first tour of Scotland was with the late Mr David Thomson, for whom and his wife, Violet Davidson, I had the greatest admiration and respect. Just at the moment I do not recollect anything that happened on this tour that would be of particular interest to my readers, except perhaps the dodge we used to adopt to keep a train compartment to ourselves. To realise their ulterior aim, the party did not scruple to use the old man of the company; that's me. Their plan was to enwrap my face and head in a huge red-flannel bandage, with instructions to sit at the window next station platforms, and so contort my physiognomy that would-be intruders, catching a glimpse of the "face at the window" hesitated, and went elsewhere in the train.

I also went on a few summer tours with Mr Donald Munro, O.B.E., whose company included Miss Lizzie Hunter, of Saltcoats, who subsequently became his wife. On one of these tours the company also included Findlater, the Dargai Piper hero, whose recourse to the platform for a living caused a great sensation at the time.

The man who really brought me to the front, however, was Mr William Walker, of Aberdeen, with whom I toured for thirteen weeks. It wasn't an unlucky number for me, for the tour firmly established my popularity and reputation in Scotland.

In those days travelling was not the "de luxe" affair it is to-day, and many a time we had to journey all night to get to our destination, and arrived more dead than alive to give our entertainment. An example will be interesting.

We would leave Aberdeen at 6.45 am, play St Andrew's Hall, Glasgow, in the afternoon; Greenock Town Hall at night; get back to Glasgow about 11.45 pm, and, leaving Glasgow next morning about seven, would reach Aberdeen about 11 am. Frequently there was no train available to take us to our next venue, and we would have to drive a certain part of the journey in order to gain Inverness, whence, by means of a horse-drawn brake, we would cover the twenty miles to Glen Urquhart.

However, despite the jostling and the inconvenience, we never wearied. What with stories and a bit lilt on the fiddle when I was in the mood, and meeting many people on the way who knew me but whom I didn't know, time invariably passed pleasantly and rapidly.

Strenuous Times

When I travelled with Mr William Walker's Company, the country towns did not have the convenient and commodious halls they boast now-a-days, and many a time and oft we had to fit up a tent (begged, borrowed, or stolen!) or commandeer a barn in which to give our "show." Even on occasions we improvised a stage in a fish shed, in which the fishermen and women would stand for two hours and more without a murmur. Catch an audience doing that nowadays! They turn up their noses if they don't get a cushioned seat for sixpence!

Despite the discomforts of the sitting accommodation in the old days, I have known people drive forty miles in a gig in a blinding snow-storm, and stand during the whole performance, simply because they wanted to hear me play *Bovaglie's Plaid*, *The Cradle Song*, *The Laird o' Drumblair*, and *The Atholl Highlanders*.

Mr Walker was a considerate manager, and always did everything possible for our comfort. The appearances of his company on Deeside, when Royalty had forgathered there, were numerous, and frequently we

Mr William Walker, with whose company
Scott Skinner toured.

had the honour and privilege of performing to personages of high degree at Balmoral, Braemar, and Ballater. On such occasions my compositions were in great demand, for Deeside was a stronghold of mine.

A humorous incident that occurred at Falkirk is well worth recounting. It was the custom to open the show with a short pictorial entertainment, consisting of a few "still" lantern slides, generally of an educative character. One of the very best slides we had was of a little Cupid who was depicted on the screen as a previous snow-storm was dissolving.

By some mischance at Falkirk a fly had got into the lantern lens, and, magnified considerably, it was seen buzzing around Cupid's body. This strange spectacle quite excited a wee chap in the audience. Jumping up from his seat, the Falkirk bairn, pointing to the screen, shrieked excitedly—"Flap it wi' yer bunnet, laddie; flap it wi' yer bunnet—quick."

The whole audience simply rocked with laughter, and a serious picture was transformed into a screaming farce by the lad's action.

"Robin" Rejected

An incident that happened at Motherwell will bear recapitulation. Miss Lizzie Hunter had been to the platform, and the unexpected happened when she failed to evoke an encore, for Lizzie was most popular all over Scotland. I followed Lizzie to the platform, and, as usual, prepared for an encore by laying the music for *Auld Robin Gray* at the top of the platform steps.

But the fate that had overtaken Lizzie Hunter also awaited me. That audience in Motherwell was the most flint-like I ever encountered, and I retired encoreless. Stopping at the head of the stairs, where Miss Hunter had stood listening, I picked up my music, with the doleful remark—"Puir Auld Robin—ye're no' wantit—come awa' hame!" Miss Hunter (now Mrs Donald Munro), nearly split her sides laughing at the remark.

While we were on the way down to Campbeltown, a lady member of the party, while in the grip of mal-de-mer, catapulted her artificial molars overboard, and in an abandon of excitement rushed to the bridge and demanded that the captain stop the vessel and look for her teeth. Poor girl, that whimsical request was kept up on her for many a day.

Before a performance at Stirling, I remember our party paying a visit to the Wallace Monument. About 500 yards from the bottom, when I was on the way down, one of the party who had preceded me in the descent, called back—"Let's see how you can run," and, not loath to show I was far from being a "done old man," I at once complied. When I gained on the company, I got a fright when one of them, pointing to my feet, exclaimed, "Doctor, yet fit's a' bluid." ("Doctor" was the familiar name by which I was known to my touring friends, though I cannot recollect the origin of it.)

Sure enough, when I looked, the blood was oozing through my hose. The Skean Dhu in my hose had left its socket, shot in the air, and buried itself deep in my ankle after penetrating my gaiter.

I hirpled to a chemist to have the wound dressed. It was very painful, but I comforted myself with the reflection that, like Wallace, I had bled for Scotland!

Misfortunes

This tour, as I have said, lasted thirteen weeks, and was highly successful. At the time I never attached any superstitious significance to the number 13, and when certain members of the party would be quibbling over the rooms they were to occupy in hotels, I would boldly offer to occupy Room 13 in defiance of all traditions and superstitions.

Since those days, however, I have had quite a number of experiences which tend to confirm the unlucky associations of this number, and now I wouldn't sit down to dinner in a company of thirteen for anything.

I need not recall all the incidents which lead to this resolution. One will suffice. This happened in Dundee, where I found myself in room 13 of a hotel there.

I could not have been more than a couple of minutes in the room when disaster overtook me. A huge wardrobe stood in the room, and I began to open the glass door of this to put my fiddle inside out of harm's way. I had just opened the door about six inches, when the top-piece of the wardrobe, without the slightest warning, descended like an Alpine avalanche. Luckily the heavy piece of wood missed me, but it was only by an inch or so. Had it struck me on the head, the story of my life would have been written by others, for I should have been a "gone coon!" Never again will I occupy no.13 room in any hotel. I'd rather risk an eightpenny or "bob doss" in a "model."

The party at this time included Miss Dolly Donaldson, of Aberdeen, a beautiful contralto singer, who also acted as accompanist. Dolly was the life and soul of the party, and was very fond of a joke.

At Stirling, I remember, the company were all busy dressing for the platform. Dolly, in order to expedite her toilet, swung round the gas jet towards me, and the next instant the smell of burning or singeing near to my own nostrils caused me to put my hands to my cranium, to discover that the seat of the "fire" was actually there. My hair at the time was about five inches long, but by the time I had arrested the singeing process, it was a good deal shorter.

Dolly, instead of expressing her regret, burst out laughing, and when I remonstrated with her, she merely said, "Oh, Doctor, you looked so comical that I could do nothing but laugh!"

I can laugh now, but I didn't feel like laughing then. I am afraid I "lost my wool" in more senses than one.

Seven

A Visit to the Orkneys—Our Eventful Voyage—Enthusiasm at Kirkwall

MY FIRST MEETING WITH GEORGE WALKER, the well-known Scottish vocalist (now of the Music Hall Cinema, Aberdeen), was at Edinburgh in 1896. The company on that occasion, it is worthwhile noting, consisted of Mary Burnett, a well-known soprano; Jessie Gainmont, a distinguished contralto; Robert Kennedy, tenor, one of the famous Kennedy family; George Walker, the renowned baritone; Donald Munro, the popular O.B.E., of Banchory, elocutionist; and myself.

I well remember hearing Mr Walker sing *The Macgregor's Gathering, Hurrah for the Highlands*, and *The March of the Cameron Men*. I was drawn to him both as a singer and a man, and we fraternised in the hotel after the concert. This was the beginning of a leal friendship that is strong and true to this day.

After supper Walker, Kennedy, Munro, and I adjourned to the smoke-room, and whiled away an hour or two in story-telling, and here I formed the opinion that George Walker was one of the finest raconteurs I had ever met. His stories on this occasion were simply irresistible, in addition to which his intense love of everything Scottish warmly commended his personality to me.

The friendship thus begun was destined to bear excellent fruit a few years later, when I set out on my first tour with Mr Robert Calder, of Aberdeen (now residing in Fraserburgh), for whom Mr George Walker acted as manager.

I was in Glasgow, where I had been playing to one of the 'Shire Highland Associations, when I received a telegram from Mr Walker asking me if I would go on a tour with Mr Calder's company. In those days I was very particular about the composition of the companies I joined, and I wired back asking for the names of the other artistes. This information, when supplied, showed that I was asked to join what was then without a doubt the strongest company touring Scotland. The personnel was Jessie Maclachlan, the great soprano prima-donna; George Neil, the brilliant Scottish tenor; Jessie G. Robertson, the famous Scottish contralto; Davie Thomson, the well-known comedian; George Walker; Robert Buchanan, pianist; and myself, for, of course, when I learned of the cast, I had no hesitation in joining the concern. In addition, Mr Calder gave a cinematograph entertainment, which was then in its infancy, and was regarded as a world's wonder by country folks.

Again our travelling facilities were oft-times of the most primitive description. Three sea journeys especially stand out in bold relief. We were due to appear at Kirkwall, in the Orkney Islands, and we were to have left Scrabster at four o'clock in the afternoon.

As luck would have it, we missed the *St Ola*, the steamer that was to have taken us across, but, nothing daunted, Mr Calder hunted around to see if there was any kind of sea-worthy craft available to make a special voyage.

Curious Craft

As a result, a special boat (emphasis on the "special!") was chartered. It was a delapidated looking steamer, the most horrible craft in which I ever sailed.

All its blemishes, however, were not discernable until we were well out to sea. We left at midnight, and three hours were regarded as ample for the voyage. It was a beautiful moonlit night when we cast off from Scrabster, all of us in the best of spirits at the solution of our transport problem by having a whole boat to ourselves.

But exploration of the craft soon disillusioned us. As for the smoke-room, eg the engine room, the male members had to make their visits there one at a time.

Still, it was quite sufficient for all the demands we made upon it, for there were few among us who could even contemplate the idea of a smoke shortly after our barque had heaved off from the quay.

We were not long out in the open sea when a veritable hurricane arose. Our little vessel commenced to bob about on the billows like the proverbial cockle-shell, and if ever I prayed strenuously and sincerely it was that night. And the urgent desire of my prayer was "Land, land, land!"

I was never much of a sailor, and, of course, mal-de-mer was to be expected. Fellow-sufferers will have a fellow-feeling, and I need not attempt to describe my sensations. I clung tenaciously to the taffrail while I gave back to the sea its own. (I had had a fish supper before setting sail!) Such was my dire plight when a man (he must have been a member of the crew) approached and made the most diabolically inane remark ever addressed to me.

"Are ye seek, sir?" said he.

Despite my nausea, I felt like throwing the questioner overboard, but contented myself with the reply in as bitter tones as my aching throat would permit— "Naw; I'm only doin' this for fun!"

Mr George Walker, Aberdeen, with whom Mr Scott Skinner was often associated.

Three hours, as I said before, was considered quite sufficient to take us across, but, ye gods and little fishes! the voyage lasted thirteen. An unlucky number, to be sure.

Eventful Voyages

The rest of the company, like myself, had been in the pulverising grip of sea-sickness, and we were a disreputable-looking party when we landed in time for lunch.

"Never again!" exclaimed Jessie Maclachlan, but, in spite of this resolution, the greatest vocalist that Scotland ever saw or heard repeated the journey to the Orkneys many times—under more pleasant conditions than those I have described, I hope.

It is astonishing how soon one forgets one's trials and troubles. Even the memory of sea-sickness can be obliterated by a few hours ashore, and sometimes even enjoyed—in the retrospect. So it was with us, but it wasn't long till we experienced an adventure akin to that narrated above.

Between the Orkneys and the Shetland Islands there is a strip of water known as "The Roost," where a number of currents are supposed to meet.

After giving a highly successful "show" at Kirkwall, we set sail in the well-known North of Scotland and Orkney Island Steam Navigation Company's steamer, *The Queen*, for the Shetland Islands.

If the crossing to Kirkwall was bad, this voyage simply "put the lid on it." Stormy was not the name for the conditions when we cast off. The wind howled and whistled, and the little vessel rose on waves that were literally mountains high, to dip down into the watery abysses from which it seemed impossible for her ever to rise.

Our party was undoubtedly panicky, and wished they had never left land. I clambered on the bridge before sea-sickness came again to flatten me out, and, bawling into the captain's ear, nervously asked him what was likely to happen.

The old "salt" shrugged his shoulders, and shouted back to me— "There's ae consolation—we're just aboot a couple o' miles frae lan'." For all the difference that fact made, I believed the distance might as well have been a hundred miles, for had the vessel foundered not one of us, I'm certain, would have been saved.

"Ye'll be a' richt, onyway," shouted the skipper, trying to maintain a conversation in spite of the storm.

"How?" said I curiously.

"Och, ye'll can strap yerself to yer fiddle-box an' float ashore!"

Seething Cauldron

From Lerwick we went down to Scalloway, where, after our "show," we had time and no more to catch the steamship *St Clair* for Stromness. Once more the Firth was a seething cauldron, and a number of the company were disinclined to embark and risk another bout of sea-sickness. The captain, however, assured them that the conditions were not quite so bad as they seemed, and the entire party came aboard.

We left at 10.30 pm, and out in the open once more, the vessel, we learned, was hardly getting out of the bit, so fierce was the storm raging. Thus we were buffeted about without making any headway for about six hours, and we didn't reach Stromness till 9.30 the following evening.

It only wanted a few minutes to ten o'clock by the time we disembarked, and our concert was advertised to begin at eight. A tremendous crowd stood on the quay awaiting our arrival, and a gruff voice as we drew alongside called out—"Is Scott Skinner aboard?" I was in no mood for answering frivolous questions, but my friend, Mr George Walker, bellowed out—"Aye, he's had the time o' his life, and he's simply itchin' tae play tae ye—I don't think!"

The crowd thronged around us when we disembarked, and pelted questions at us about the concert. We had made up our minds that there was to be no "show" that night. The night was well spent—and so were we, but so persistent were the Stromnessians that, after a rapid consultation, we decided to give a sort of impromptu performance in a neighbouring goods-shed, and there the people of this outlandish spot heard me play the fiddle for the very first time.

Although the environment was far from congenial (I stood on a box so that I should be seen), and sea-sickness had left me in a very "weeshy-washy" condition, I know I did not play badly, and the reception I received could not have been bettered by the musical clientele that forgathers in Albert or Queen's Hall, London.

It is no exaggeration to say that these Stromnessians, about whom there was no veneer or sophistication, simply went wild with delight, and they would have kept me playing till the "sma' 'oors" if I had been so inclined.

This was my first visit to the Orkney and Shetland Islands, and at the time I made up my mind it was to be my last, but, like Jessie Maclachlan, I went back again, in spite of all the discomforts I had suffered, and on these occasions—with Father Neptune in a more amicable mood—I really enjoyed the trips.

The people of these islands, I might add, are very keen critics and excellent listeners, and I was always at home among them. They were quick to appreciate real talent, and as quick, I learned from certain reports, to show their disapproval of a spurious article.

Rousing Reception

When I made my first appearance at Kirkwall, the hall was packed to overflowing, and many clamouring for admission had to be turned away. Hundreds were content with standing room so long as they could hear Jessie Maclachlan and "The Strathspey King". Jessie's songs in Gaelic were tremendously popular.

One of my solos at this time introduced *The Atholl Highlanders*, *The Balmoral Highlanders*, and *The Queen's Welcome to Invercauld*—pipe tunes that have never been bettered even up till the present day—and this solo was a huge favourite in Orkney and Shetland.

When I had played it at Kirkwall the people sprang to their feet like a platoon "shunned" by the regimental sergeant-major, and for a time the scene in the hall was pandemonium. But it was not only myself they took to their hearts.

Jessie Maclachlan, one of the sweetest women I have ever known, brought the tears to their eyes with her great number, *Can You Sew Cushions?* and then had them in an ecstasy of excitement with a thrilling and powerful rendering of *A Hundred Pipers*.

On the programme I followed Jessie, and before I stepped on to the platform George Walker whispered in my ear, "My word,'King', ye've something tae dae tae follow her." But, as already observed, my reception was equally boisterous and heartening.

Some time later I went on tour with Mr George Walker when he took to the road with a party of his own. This was indeed a pleasant interlude in my life, for Mr Walker, though a much younger man than myself, had more experience in concert work, and he was in a way practically a father to me. At all events, he was my "guide, philosopher, and friend," and he knows I appreciated all his kindness and consideration.

Mr Walker has one characteristic which many another manager would do well to cultivate. He would tolerate no undue interference from anyone, and kept outsiders out of the "green room" as much as possible, on the ground that their presence was not in the best interests of the artistes or of the programme.

There are always a number of people who like to thrust themselves into the artistes' room before the concert commences, and, as I have found personally, it is a most irritating practice.

The "champing" of feet while I was playing was also a nuisance, and Mr Walker thought to stop it by the announcement—"Please keep time with the rhythm with the toe inside your boot. You will find it has the same effect." This invariably tickled the audience, and there was seldom reason

A little group of Mr Scott Skinner and his friends, taken while he was appearing in charity concerts on Deeside.

for complaint after the request had been made.

My first visit to the Vale of Leven was in the nature of a triumphal march. At Dumbarton and Alexandria the attentions of my admirers were really irksome, though flattering. Quite a crowd awaited me at Dumbarton Station on one occasion. They had never seen me before, but my reputation, both as a player and a composer, had preceded my visit in the flesh.

"Vale" Hero-Worship

Mr Walker and I walked together, and, unconscious of the fact that we were the cause of the crowd, we wandered up the main street, to find that the crowd followed us. Whenever we stopped at a shop window we were immediately surrounded, and there was a clamour to shake hands with me.

I was absolutely bewildered, and when I had complied with a number of requests for a handshake Mr Walker and I moved on, but still the crowd followed, and at length we decided on precipitate flight to escape them.

Alexandria Co-Operative Society at this time ran the Saturday evening concerts, and when I proceeded there I remember a deputation of the Committee of the Society called upon me, even before the concert, and asked me if I would appear at one of their Saturday concerts.

"Surely you're not going to engage a man you've never heard play," I temporised.

"Oh, yes, we have heard you play," replied the spokesman. "We were up at Dumbarton last night and heard you. The Committee held a rapid consultation this morning, and it was unanimously decided to ask you to come to one of our Saturday night concerts."

I was pleased, yea, flattered, and I promised to try and make an appearance at one of their concerts. This, however, I was unable to do, for the simple reason that I had prior engagements with Mr Calder and Mr Walker to fulfil there. I fully appreciated the kindness of the Alexandria Co-Operators in offering me an engagement, and I trust if any of them chance to read these lines they will accept my excuse as valid and genuine. The Co-Operative Society concerts in those days were a power in the land, and nothing would have given me greater pleasure than to play for them.

Old Duncan M'Vean, Allan M'Lennan, Walter Calder, and Miss Johnston, of the Albert Hotel—all were well-known figures in Alexandria, and great friends of mine in those days, and whenever I struck their little town they gave me of their best hospitality. The majority, if not all, of them are gone now, and it makes me sad to reflect that I am now about the only one left.

Eight

The Troubles of the Caledonian Four—Funny Experiences in Aberdeenshire

WHEN MY TOURS WITH Mr George Walker came to an end, Harry (now Sir Harry) Lauder suggested that a picked party of four should attempt to take London by storm. I ought to have mentioned that I had previously met Harry while doing holiday tours with Mr Donald Munro. Harry and George Walker were great friends, hence the suggestion by the former.

I happened to be in Fraserburgh along with Mr Walker when Lauder's letter was forwarded. George and I discussed the project at considerable length, and realised, like the Yankee, that it was "some proposeetion," but comforted ourselves with the reflection that help from an artiste with a reputation like Harry Lauder might mean all the difference between success and failure, for at this time Sir Harry was at the zenith of his power and popularity in London. Anything he proposed to Metropolitan managers invariably carried weight and conviction and was certain of a good hearing.

Bearing this in mind, we felt that the project was not to be lightly tackled, and we took some time to arrive at a decision, for we had an unholy dread of "letting down" our sponsor.

However, having considered the proposal from every possible point of view, we decided that we were equal to the task, with the assistance of other two capable artistes.

On our last tour we had a young lady named Miss Jeanie Hendry, Scotland's champion international dancer, who had taken first prize eight years in succession at Braemar. Said Mr Walker to me: "It would be quite a good idea if we could get some part in which to introduce Miss Hendry, as, I am sure, her dancing would be an innovation in the halls."

I agreed, for I had a great opinion of Jeanie's abilities (she is now a dancing mistress in Aberdeen), and Mr Walker there and then decided to include her in the company, which blossomed out under the cognomen of *The Caledonian Four.*

Never a procrastinator, George sat down forthwith to write a sketch called *The Outlaw,* set in the troubled days of Flora Macdonald and Bonnie Prince Charlie. Then we secured the services of Miss Jeannie Middleton, the well-known soprano, and the quartette which was to assail the Metropolis was complete. Miss Middleton was also to fill the role of pianist.

In the sketch I was a laird, George Walker was my son, Miss Hendry my kitchenmaid, and Miss Middleton a guest of mine. It was conveyed to the public by a little prologue that the laird had just enabled Bonnie Prince Charlie to escape his pursuers, and after my exciting exertions, I was sitting having a "nap" at the fireside. The curtain went up to reveal this "sleepy" scene.

Caught "Not Napping"

Rehearsals were held in the banqueting hall of the Royal Hotel, Aberdeen, and went on for three weeks. Everything went smoothly, and then Harry Lauder appeared in the Palace Theatre, Aberdeen. Having been informed that his proposal had been adopted, he took the opportunity of seeing the sketch acted.

After a little pruning and a little advice by himself (very valuable indeed), he pronounced the "show" fit for any Metropolitan stage.

It was then we discussed the question of a name for the party, and Lauder's suggestion of *The Caledonian Four* was adopted, and, having painted our own scenery, we set out full of faith and hope, trusting possibly to the audiences to be charitable in their criticism.

We got our first engagement at the Palladium in London. As a matter of fact, we had the honour of opening that famous hall. On the same bill were Mr Matheson Lang and his wife (Miss Huton Britton),

Sir Harry Lauder, who gave the concert party valuable assistance in producing thei· sketch.

so we realised that we must be on our mettle.

The best way of indicating how our sketch "went down" is to quote from an account which was wired to a Scottish evening newspaper. This read—

"*The Caledonian Four* gave a musical and dramatic scena, with setting and scenery by Harry Lauder. The dramatic element, it was obvious, served merely to introduce high-class music. Mr Walker led off with a spirited rendering of *Macgregors' Gathering*, his resonant voice serving him well in the huge auditorium. He was followed by Miss Hendry, who performed excellent Highland dances to the music of the band, after which Miss Middleton treated the audience to a tasteful rendering of *There's a Wee Bit Land*.

"The triumph of the evening, however, was left to Mr Scott Skinner, who treated the audience to a brilliant display on the violin. The appreciation of the audience reached its climax when the veteran danced a step or two to his own strathspeys and reels. The whole turn, which concluded with *Auld Lang Syne*, was received with the utmost cordiality."

When the scene opened with the singing of *Will Ye No' Come Back Again?* (the Prince just having been smuggled away), I was supposed to be asleep in an easy chair by the fireside. On the opening night, however, the lifting of the curtain caught me—not "napping!"—but in the act of lighting my pipe.

Quick as thought, I flung myself into the chair and fell fast asleep in record time, just as from the lips of George Walker fell the words—"Hush, the Laird's asleep!"

Smart as I thought I had been in retrieving the situation, the audience were too quick for me. Unrestrained laughter broke loose and in George Walker's own words, "when he looked across, instead of seeing me sleeping, I was sitting amused and smiling," thus endangering our first appearance in London which we had intended to take by storm.

A Big Fright

George Walker, always prepared for such situations, promptly straightened out the tangle by turning round and remarking to the two ladies—"it is just as well he isn't asleep. We will get him to join in the festivities on this night, presumably our last, in the old home."

At this point a summons is served. The audience, getting interested and desisting from laughter, George Walker reads out the summons which is to the effect that the Laird (that's me!) is to be arrested and imprisoned for his underhand work in smuggling the Prince out of the country.

Being asleep, I was not supposed to hear this, but, missing the idea of the camouflage, I jumped up and anxiously enquired—

"When do I play?"

Without answering me, George Walker proceeded—"Although the Macgregors are involved in this charge of treason, 'Macgregors, despite them, shall flourish for ever'," and precluded any further interruption from me by bursting into a rousing rendering of *The Macgregors' Gathering.*

Despite this little contretemps, the show proved a most successful one. Among those present were Sir Harry and Lady Lauder, who duly congratulated us on our success.

But I had almost forgotten to tell you that during this same performance I had a very narrow escape of being seriously injured. An elastic band inside my kilt was responsible. In the course of the "show" I did a few steps of the Highland Fling, and everything went merry and bright till the heel of my uplifted shoe caught the elastic band, and precipitated me in the direction of the orchestra. But suddenly the elastic band snapped, and released my entangled slipper, otherwise I should have fallen headlong among the orchestra and been seriously injured. As it was, I picked myself up little the worse, and carried on. I got a big fright, however.

A Late Entry

From London we went to Lewisham, where our appearance was also marked by a singular occurrence. The tramcar in which we were travelling was held up for some reason, and as we were likely to be late by walking, Mr Walker (no pun intended!), who had to get various things in order for the start, dashed off at top speed, leaving me to come on alone. The ladies had left earlier than Mr Walker and I.

I had no earthly idea where the hall was, but after a good deal of wandering and "speirin'," I discovered the place, only to find, to my consternation, that my three co-artistes were on the platform, and that Mr Walker was in the middle of his rendering of *The Macgregors' Gathering.*

Now here was a problem. How was I to get on in a perfectly natural and legitimate way and without being conspicuous? All manner of subterfuges entered my head, but, harassed as I was by the fix I had put myself and the others in, I couldn't think them out to finality.

Immediately George Walker finished his song, I was supposed to spring up from the chair in which I had been dozing, and exclaim—"Bravo!" That was impracticable now, but without any definite scheme, I slipped out

The Caledonian Four concert party, whose adventures are so graphically
described.

of the wings as Walker finished, and, shaking him by the hand,
exclaimed—"Well done!" and in a whisper to the singer—"Hoo did ye
manage it?"

"I simply presumed you were there," he explained in a hurried sotto
voice, "and made known the fact that we were preparing to have a night of it
in the old home. Your coming in and saying 'Well done' saved the
situation."

It was a near thing, but it was providential that I made my entry at the
time I did, as almost every agent in London was there that night to hear us.

Immediately after this show we beat back to Aberdeen, where we had
an outbreak of fire to add spice to our entertainment. The house was
packed to the door. I had just stepped on to the platform when the word
"Fire!" of awful significance in a crowded building, was shrieked.

I looked round and saw the wings in flames, then, glancing at the
auditorium, beheld panic on the faces of the audience. And the stampede
for the exits began.

Fire Alarm

I was convinced that the fire would be got under control before it could reach the main part of the hall, so, thinking to calm the people and avert the tragedy that might be caused by their own rashness, I signalled to the band and shouted—"play up the *Birlin' Reels*," which, by the way, was not the solo I had selected for my turn.

Then, stepping nearer to the footlights, I addressed the panic-stricken people, "There is no cause for alarm," I said. "The flames are well in hand," and I proceeded to play the famous *Birlin' Reels* with all the verve and vivacity at my command.

The audience, seeing and hearing me play, halted in their panic-stricken and dangerous scramble, convinced if it was safe for me, it must also be safe for them. By the time I had finished the reels, the flames had been completely extinguished, and the ovation I received from the people, I believe, was more for my successful efforts to calm them than because of any merit in my playing.

A little presence of mind, that was all, but I was assured that it prevented accident, if not tragedy. Many a kiddie might have been trampled on had I not stepped forward and given them *The Birlin' Reels*. Which goes to prove the truth of the saying that "Music hath power to soothe the savage beast."

Dundee was our next place of call, and a wonderful reception we received in the King's Theatre.

Nothing of note took place during this performance, but in the afternoon prior to our appearance I overheard a rather amusing conversation. This was at the corner of Dock Street, where there is, or used to be, a pillar-box with a big blue cap decorated with a red band.

Two rustic chiels bent on seeing Dundee playing the Edinburgh Hearts at Dens Park, were gazing at the pillar-box when I approached. I halted and listened, for I was sure I would hear something original, and perhaps funny, and I did.

"Man, Tam," said one to the other, "that's a queer thing. Whit wad that be for, noo?"

"Dod," replied Tam, "I've nae idea, but I'm thinkin' by the look o't it's something tae dae wi' the Salvation Army."

"Na, na," chimed in the other, "it's naethin' tae dae wi' the Salvation Army ava, Tam."

"And hoo d'ye mak' that oot?" queried Tam.

"Look, man," was the reply, and a finger was directed at the printed plate giving a list of collections and deliveries, "it says—'nae collections on Sundays!'"

In Dundee I renewed many old friendships. Never in my life did I receive so many invitations to dine. I could not accept them all, but I fully appreciated the kindness of the Dundonians.

The Tour Ends

In the Glasgow Alhambra we had another triumph. It is pathetic to recall that this was the last occasion on which I had a tete-a-tete with my dear old friend Willie Frame. "The Man U Know" shook me warmly by the hand, and remarked—"Man, Skinner, ye're an auld man (I was 66 then), an' I hope Scotland appreciates the fact that you've done more to keep her muse alive than anyone else I know."

Poor Willie! As I was a good bit older than he was, he never dreamt that he would be "off the carpet" before me, but I am still "on the carpet" and on the platform, while the voice of one of the wittiest and most enterprising entertainers Scotland ever produced is forever stilled.

While travelling from Glasgow to London, where we were due to appear in the Alhambra (my last appearance in a music hall, by the way), my friend, George Walker, contracted a very bad cold. On the Sunday morning he was very hoarse, and a doctor who was called in declared he had a touch of bronchitis, adding that his appearance in the Alhambra the following evening was out of the question.

George, however, would not hear of the "show" proceeding without him, and, with a temperature of 103, went on to play and sing as usual.

We tried hard to dissuade him, but he was inflexible. His indomitable spirit asserted itself, and he went on and sang *The Macgregors' Gathering* in better style and voice than I had ever previously heard him.

But he paid the penalty. For six weeks he was laid up in London, and the career of *The Caledonian Four* came to an end, and I went back to fulfil individual engagements in Scotland.

In the middle of our London season came the Coronation of King George, and the four of us were in great demand in private houses in the West End, where the ruling spirits were Scots.

One of my greatest friends at that time (he's still my friend) was Dr (now Sir) James Cantlie, the eminent Harley Street specialist, who was born and brought up in Dufftown. *The Caledonian Four* spent a merry night under his hospitable roof, and from that day till now Sir James, who is a great lover of strathspeys, and I have corresponded regularly.

Portrait Presented

While referring to Sir James Cantlie, it would not be amiss to mention that he was the means of having painted the portrait of me which now adorns a wall of the Albert Institute, Dundee.

It was on a subsequent visit to London that I learned that a painter, Mr J. Young Hunter, had been commissioned to make a portrait of me. I was introduced to him in the Great Northern Hotel, and it was only after he had followed me all over the place, studying my physiognomy, that I learned the secret.

Several years later the presentation took place in the Music Hall, Edinburgh, in the presence of about 1500 people. Dr Cantlie, as he was then, made a very eulogistic speech, which I needn't trouble to quote, but I assure you the occasion was a very proud one in my life.

To return to my life proper, I now found myself much in demand all over the country as a solo violinist, and a few of the incidents that happened at various concerts may be worth recalling.

After an appearance at Maud, two farmers, who had driven in from the New Deer district to hear me, were overheard discussing my abilities.

"An' fit d'ye think o' yon fiddler, Sandy?" said one, who knew me, to the other, who apparently didn't.

"Aw," was the answer, "I dinna ken muckle aboot it, but yon man Scott Skinner—"

"It's him I'm speakin' aboot, man."

"Weel, there's naething in Scott Skinner's heid but meesic, but ma heid's jist fu' o' beasts!"

While touring with Mr George Walker I might have mentioned that I had the questionable honour of holding up a train. No, I didn't turn bandit. I did it in quite a "lawful" fashion.

The incident happened at a place which perforce shall be nameless, but it will be evident that it was on the North of Scotland Railway. At this station the engine took in water, and I asked if I would have time to take a run down to the village and see an old friend who kept a hotel.

"Ay, ay," said the guard, "but dinna be langer than ten meenites. The North train gangs by then, an' we'll be gettin' awa'!" (I ought to explain that the line was single, with a loop at certain stations.)

From the hotel door I could see a long stretch of the line, and decided that I would be safe to await the passing of the northbound train. A quarter of an hour passed, but I didn't worry. However, having finished my chat with my old friend, I began a leisurely dander back to the station. Suddenly I became aware of a tremendous commotion in that quarter. A bell rang clamorously, and I saw the stationmaster and porter gesticulating frantically, but, unconscious of the reason of the furore, I didn't quicken my pace in the least.

But when I sauntered on to the platform I was roughly caught by the guard and bundled into the nearest compartment without a word of explanation, and while I was picking myself off the floor the train steamed off.

Having collected my wits and taken the dust off my kilt, I calmly enquired of a fellow-passenger the cause of it all. He told me that the engine had been "watered" quite ten minutes.

"But the North train's no' passed yet," said I.

"Na," said he, "a telegram cam' in tae say it wis held up faurer doon, an' we're tae gane on, an' pass it at —— ."

Scott Skinner was thus the means of keeping two trains ten minutes later than they need have been, which may or may not prove that a prophet has some honour in his own country!

Nine

A Hard Day's Work—My Greatest London Triumph—When I "Murdered the Pianist"

MY FIRST APPEARANCE IN GLASGOW would be made about thirty years ago, and so successful did it prove that I was induced to make many return visits, which, as a matter of fact, still continue.

It was in the Second City of the Empire, whose citizens have always evinced a warm affection for me, which I fully reciprocate, that the hardest day's work I ever got through as a public performer was accomplished.

I was booked by Mr Walter Freer, one of the most courteous gentlemen I ever met, to appear at three Corporation recitals on the same Saturday afternoon. After dressing in a hotel, I took a cab to the City Hall, where I played to 4000 people.

Thence I drove to the National Hall (since demolished), on the South Side, and entertained an audience of some 2000, and finished up in St Andrew's Hall (Charing Cross) before 5000 people.

With the hall clock at fourteen minutes to five, I still held the platform, and had my train to catch to Dundee (where I was due for an evening concert) at five o'clock at Buchanan Street Station.

Making my acknowledgements as punctiliously as possible under the circumstances, which meant the spurning of another encore, I dashed off the platform. Mr Walter Freer, eager to help me, had a cab waiting at the door, and slipped the fee I had earned into my hand as I darted for the waiting vehicle.

"Drive as you never drove before!" I shouted to the man on the "dicky" as I plunged headlong into the cab. Had there been taxis then, there would have been no excuse for excitement or flurry, but some nine minutes to do the journey from St Andrew's Hall to Buchanan Street Station in a horse-drawn cab—well, it couldn't be other than exciting for the man who was bent on catching the train.

Happily, I did catch it and kept my engagement. There were no dining-cars on the trains in those days, so I wired a Dundee hotel, and when I arrived at the Gilfillan Hall, the "boots" was in attendance with tea and biscuits, which I swallowed hastily before going on to play to an audience some 1300 strong.

That, believe me, was the hardest day's work I ever did in my life, and even were I thirty or forty years younger than I am to-day, I should not be induced on any account to repeat it.

Four different halls (one of them eighty miles from the others), and solos to over 12,000 people within the space of seven hours! Looking back on that memorable Saturday, I still feel disposed to perspire—or expire!

A Tartan Triumph

In all, I must have made a score of appearances in London. To conquer the metropolis has been the dominating ambition of artistes for many a decade. Let them but get a foothold before the footlights in London, and the future, think they, is thereafter one long and happy vista of success for them. This attitude of course, is very complimentary to the citizens of the metropolis, but I am not at all sure that the encomium is justified. For my honest opinion is that, in many respects, a London audience is much more easily pleased than an audience in either Edinburgh, Glasgow, Dundee, or Aberdeen. But so long as London holds out the bigger salaries for artistes, musical or histrionic, so long, I suppose, will the tacit compliment be paid.

For the life of me I cannot remember at the moment when and where I made my first appearance before a London audience. While I have said "London audience," I should add that my audiences there were generally mostly composed of Scots, and they are not easily pleased, whether in Toronto or Timbuctoo!

All my London visits, it is no exaggeration to say, were triumphs, but if I were asked to indicate the occasion on which I thought my reception was most uproariously flattering, it would be when I appeared in the Albert Hall and played before a packed house. It was a Scottish gathering, pure and undefiled.

In the first part of the programme I appeared in the Gordon kilt. My

A charming study of Miss Jeannie Hendry, who has often danced to Scott Skinner's playing in concert engagements.

reception was cordial in the extreme, but when I marched on in the second half, arrayed in the Macpherson tartan, to which I had changed because I was going to play *Macpherson the Freebooter*, the scene was pandemonium in the most complimentary sense of the term.

The Macphersons must have been out en masse that night, and it wasn't long till those who didn't belong to this great clan contracted Macphersonitis, for before I had started to play my solo the whole audience seemed to be on their feet cheering frantically.

Clothes make the man, it is said, and I have no hesitation in saying that the Macpherson tartan made a large contribution to my gigantic success that night.

My reception on appearing was only equalled by the applause I received when I had finished my rendering of *Macpherson the Freebooter*, and here, I should think, it will be interesting to give the history of this famous air.

An Ancient Tune

Macpherson, "the Freebooter", is said to have composed this tune while awaiting execution in Banff some 45 years before Culloden. He gave a copy of it to his jailer, who passed it on to his son, who, in turn, handed it to a William Forbes, a "bricker" (a maker of bricks), in Ellon. He latterly gifted it to the late Mr Wm. M'Combie Smith, from whom I got it.

There was no authentic copy of it till I published the air, but many "chapman" versions of it were sung in the markets. Mr M'Combie Smith paid me a neat compliment in this connection.

"Scott Skinner," said he, "if you had done nothing else but rescue and preserve 'Macpherson the Freebooter', and 'The Braes of Auchtertyre', you would have done well."

Many stories of the prowess, daring, and love affairs of the Freebooter are still alive in the North. It was for the murder of a rival for a lady's hand and heart that he swung on the ignominious gallows-tree at Banff. His

demeanour on that inauspicious occasion is described in the words which
go to his own air—

Sae rantin'ly, sae wantonly,
Sae dauntin'ly gaed he,
He played a tune, an' danced it roon
Below the gallows-tree!

About twenty years ago, when I was living at Monikie, near Dundee,
along with my second wife (Gertrude Mary Anderton Park Skinner), I went
to London, accompanied by her. In Dundee, before setting out, we heard
the great Kubelik in the Kinnaird Hall, and at the close the renowned
violinist and I had an interesting conversation, in which we indulged in
mutual congratulations.

I think on this occasion I was fulfilling an engagement along with the
great Jessie Maclachlan, who was much in demand in London. Arrived in
the metropolis, we were entertained at dinner by Mr Jonathan Clarke, my
wife's solicitor, at his home at 2 Devonshire Terrace.

During dinner I was relating a number of incidents in my career, and
had just mentioned Charles Dickens as being one of my favourite authors,
when Mr Clarke remarked—"Well, if you are an admirer of Dickens, rise
and show it, for you are sitting in the very chair where the immortal
Dickens listened to rehearsals of his plays!"

Doctor Dumfounded

On another occasion, after I had been no fewer than six times on the
platform at the Albert Hall during one performance, a London doctor came
into the "green room" and asked to be introduced to me. I was 66 years of
age at the time.

"Ah," exclaimed the medico, "you're a marvellous man. Where do you
come from?"

"Aberdeenshire," I answered proudly.

"Oh," he replied, "that's where they make the likes of you, is it? Well, I
can tell you they don't make them up here, any way!"

Meantime the audience were clamouring for my return to the platform,
and as I moved off to make my seventh appearance, the doctor exclaimed—
"You've been on six times already, and you're going back again. That bates
a'!"

I knew from the last remark from what part of the kingdom the
solicitous medico hailed!

An appearance I made before the London Morayshire Club is

remembered by me because of an amusing interlude. Mr Ned Godfrey, a delightful pianoforte player, was my accompanist that night, and after playing for me in the first part of the programme, he left to play at another engagement, to return in time for my second half appearance. The audience, of course, was entirely composed of the male of the species.

When I came off the platform, I went to a little table quite close to it and away from the majority of the Clubmen and their friends. I saw one gentleman near the table I selected, but, as he appeared very reserved, I decided he wanted, like myself, to go undisturbed.

But it didn't take me many seconds to discover why this chap had been left severely alone. He was, in point of fact, well "spiffed," and while the others had steered clear of him, I deliberately went beside him, being then unaware of his condition—and disposition.

His condition I have indicated, and his disposition while "under the influence" was to imagine that he was in the market purchasing huge tracts of land. He started off by buying the whole of Rothes, and before he finished (or was finished by the drinks he quaffed between each "purchase") the whole of Aberdeenshire and a large portion of Inverness-shire had fallen under the hammer to him!

The Macintosh's Invitation

About ten years ago, while I was a guest at Drumblair, The Macintosh of Macintosh telegraphed me from London asking me to come to his residence there and play during Ascot week for the entertainment of his numerous guests.

The Macintosh had heard me playing at Dundee, and when I arrived at his London residence his piper told me that he had been talking about me ever since, and when the Ascot concert was decided on he was instructed to spare no expense to bring me down.

Other talented artistes contributed to the programme, at the conclusion of which I prepared to take my departure with them, when The Macintosh's good lady drew me aside and invited me to remain to dinner with the guests. I greatly appreciated the delicate compliment from my great countryman.

Thus I travelled a distance of about 1000 miles in order to play a few tunes to the perfervid Macintosh, but I assure you he amply repaid me for my trouble.

A visit I paid to Belfast before I became a London favourite might be chronicled here. This was along with Birrell and Lamb's Diorama of Scotland.

In Glasgow, before entraining for Greenock, I bought a gingham umbrella for eight shillings, but before I got the length of Sugaropolis I discovered that the gamp had been stolen. A notification of the loss to the stationmaster at Greenock brought no result, although I was able to fully describe the man who, I was certain, had annexed my property.

Arrived in Belfast I fixed up my lodgings, and at tea the very first night I was there, opposite me at the table, I found the very man whom I would have sworn on oath had stolen my umbrella!

The late Mr W. F. Frame, the well-known Scottish entertainer, who was a close friend of Mr Scott Skinner.

I was on the point of challenging the man (he was my landlady's husband!) on the matter, but checked the impulse, because of a fear that a cracked skull might be added to my previous misfortune. I concluded I had landed in a very "rum quarter," and that night, like the Arabs, I "folded up my tent and silently stole away," lest anything more of mine should be stolen.

When this brief tour in the North of Ireland came to a close, I remained to take up dancing classes for a period of three months. The children, in the main, were apt pupils, but one thing I remember clearly is that I couldn't get one of them to "hooch" properly.

Consternation in Strichen

Over thirty years ago I was in Strichen for a concert. I lodged in the hotel beside the bridge, and during the afternoon I was rehearsing there with a timid young man who was to be my accompanist.

The Macgregor's Gathering was to be the first item, and to improve the pianist's tempo (if not temper) I vocalised it in parts, and the fierce energy I put into the bursts of "leaves in the forest and foam on the river" made the pianist quail, and presently a servant lassie, who had been listening, dashed out of the room, and I heard her shrieking to her mistress, "Quick, mum, quick! The fiddler's murderin' the piano man!"

This reminds me of an incident in which my good friend, Mr George Rose Wood, and I were concerned. While he was lodging with an old maid at Union Grove, Aberdeen, I went at his request to give him a few hints on how to play strathspeys, but the tuition under this roof was short-lived, for the day after the second lesson the old landlady ordered Mr Wood out of the house.

"It wis bad eneuch," said she, "tae hae ae fiddler in the hoose, but I canna stand the twa o' ye, sae ye'll need tae shift. I hae aye keepit a respectable hoose, an' I'm no' for lettin' ye tak' awa' my guid name!"

And poor George had to flit!

While I was living at Monikie Mr Wood paid me several visits. On one of these occasions I was showing him round my garden, of which I was intensely and, I believe, justifiably proud. I was showing George some beautiful cabbages, when he drew my attention to a butterfly on the blade of one, remarking that the butterfly laid the eggs which produced the caterpillars which eat the cabbage.

On the impulse of the moment and in my anxiety to save my cabbage, I made a jump with the intention of annihilating the butterfly, but I was too late, and, instead of killing the butterfly, I completely destroyed two of my best cabbages. Many a good laugh George Wood has enjoyed at my expense when recalling this episode.

One of the oddest characters ever I knew was the late Forbes Morrison, who belonged to Tarves, Aberdeenshire. He belonged to the same school of fiddlers as Peter Milne and I. He could speak "Buchan" on the fiddle.

Forbes used to go to about Aberdeen dressed in the queerest fashion imaginable. He wore "tacketty" boots, a frock coat, and a "tile" hat, while a long white clay pipe seemed to eternally project from the mouth of his red-whiskered face!

Forbes took fifth prize at the Inverness competition in which I got the premier award.

In the attire I have described he used to walk the streets of Aberdeen, and I fear many of the younger generation were not indulgent of his sartorial eccentricities.

A Sensitive Ear

Of blind Willie Grant, whom I mentioned in a previous instalment, and who, like Peter Milne, was a great worthy in the North, I will give the following story. One day when I met him I was amazed to hear Willie remark—"Ye're wearin' yer kilt the day, Jimmie."

"Hoo d'ye ken, Willie?" I asked.

"Och, Jimmie," he replied with a smile, "I heard the tassels o' yer sporran reeslin'!"

Willie, like many persons bereft of sight, had a very sensitive ear. He was known for many years on the streets of Aberdeen as a player of the harmonium and a singer of Jacobite songs.

One of the most exciting adventures that ever befell me happened in Manchester about twenty-five years ago, when my son Manson accompanied me. Both of us were engaged for a concert in the Free Trade Hall. Harry (now Sir Harry) Lauder and Mrs Munro, Strathpeffer, were also contributors to the programme.

After the concert Manson and I drove in a hansom cab to our hotel. The horse was a spirited beast, which the driver had difficulty in controlling, and disaster overtook us when passing under Victoria Bridge. Here the horse, scared by the rumbling noise made by its heels under the bridge, swerved suddenly to the side, one of the wheels striking the kerb-stone.

The result was that Manson and I, after a painful collision of craniums, were sent sprawling on the narrow hansom floor, to the accompaniment of splintering glass which fell on our shoulders, luckily without hitting an exposed part.

In a tremor of excitement we both struggled out on to the street, to find the horse, whose harness had become entangled, suspended with all fours a foot from the ground. The descent of the "cabby," whose hands were cut and bleeding, relieved the tension, however, and the horse found itself once more on terra firma.

Manson was only about fifteen years of age at the time, and naturally got a big fright. So did I, as a matter of fact. I never favoured hansoms after this accident, and until the advent of the taxi-cab, thereafter bestowed my patronage on four-wheeled "growlers."

Ten

Friendship with Professor Blackie—How I Got My Fiddle

ALTHOUGH I MET HIM ONLY THRICE, the late Professor John S Blackie, one of the most distinguished and patriotic Scotsmen of his time, was, I am pleased to say, one of my staunchest friends and supporters. I owe to him a deep debt of gratitude for his labours on my behalf, which I could never hope to repay to him or his.

This friendship was faithfully fostered by correspondence, but all his letters, it is my bitter regret, have been lost. Copies of some of them, happily, exist. The following is a copy of the letter I received from him when he learned I was publishing my book, *The Harp and Claymore*—

"I am delighted to learn that you intend to favour the world with a collection of your pastoral melodies and other pieces of genuine Scottish music. There can be no doubt that of all the rich inheritance which, under Providence, Scotland has to boast of from the past, there is none more valuable than our national song and national music, and to hand down to the men of the future in all its fullness and purity this rich legacy from the past must be regarded as one of the most sacred duties of the present. Whatever beauties in music and in the fine arts may be borrowed from abroad—and no doubt there are many—there is a charm about the native product with which the foreign can no more compete than the growth of Alpine forests can rival the grace of the birch in our Scottish glens or the glory of the purple heather on the hills. Every distinct type of people has its own strong points, which it cannot neglect without paying the double penalty of weakness at home and contempt from abroad.

"With the warmest wishes for your success in the culture of our native Scottish music in all its variety."

My first meeting with the famous Professor was in Union Street, Aberdeen. I knew him at a glance. He was the most venerable and distinguished-looking figure I have ever seen.

I had sent him a number of my compositions for review, and when I saw him I availed myself of the opportunity of speaking to him on the subject.

"Oh, you're Scott Skinner!" he exclaimed, and I knew at once there was nothing hypocritical in the pleasure he evinced at our unexpected meeting.

Blackie's Blessing

"Come away," said he, and he linked his arm in mine and bore me up Union Street. In this fashion we walked up and down Aberdeen's main thoroughfare for nearly an hour, discussing things Scottish with much mutual pleasure and benefit. As we passed along numbers of people paused and stared at us, for I verily believe to the average person we were an odd-looking pair.

"D'ye ken the auld man wi' the plaid?" I heard them say.

"Naw," would come the reply.

"That's the great Professor Blackie!"

"An' the auld man he's cleekin'—fa's (who's) he?"

"That's Scott Skinner, the Strathspey King."

On this occasion I mentioned to the Professor that I proposed publishing a book of my compositions, to be known as the Logie Collection, and asked him if he would be good enough to write me an introduction. "Delighted," was the hearty response, and the following is a copy of the glowing epistle he sent me—

"I am delighted to hear that you are prosecuting vigorously your noble work of giving to the world the Logie Collection of Scottish songs, pipe tunes, Strathspeys, &c. You could not spend your genius on a task at once more patriotic and more opportune; for it is only too evident that there is a class of persons growing up in Scotland at the present hour who are willing to sacrifice the rich heritage of popular song which they have received from their fathers for exotic beauties of all descriptions, and the meretricious novelties of the hour.

"Far be it from me, brought up as I was in Germany, and breathing the inspiring atmosphere of Beethoven and Mendelssohn, to throw any discouragement on the study of musical art as presented in the masterpieces of the great German and Italian composers, but there is a peculiar charm, as well as a great moral and educative value, in all popular songs, which the most finished productions of artistic skill do not possess, and which the greatest masters of the art have often made it their greatest glory to imitate, and if popular song, or volkslied, as the Germans call it, has this special virtue, the popular music of Scotland has it in a remarkable degree; partly on account of its own excellence, partly because for we Scotsmen it has the additional advantage of being Scotch, as native to our ears and to our hearts as the purple heather is to the brae, or the graceful tresses on the birch to the glen.

"If it is true, as a wise man said, that the eyes of a fool are at the end of the earth, it is equally true that the ears of a wise man should not be tickled merely with far-sought melodies, but be turned in the first place to airs of native growth and to sounds as familiar as the breeze on the mountain or the murmur of water in the plain.

Doric Defender

"A man's first duty in nature or in art is always to his immediate surroundings, and the man who flings aside these natural sources of true culture for the worship of strange gods is both a traitor and a fool. I myself have long been profoundly convinced that, next to the Bible and the familiar aquaintance with its moral treasures that belongs to our Presbyterian piety, the Scotsman owes all that is best and most human in his character to his rich heritage of popular song; and the moment he ceases to draw inspiration from these sources he will either cease to exist altogether, absorbed in the body of John Bull, or exist only in a state of apish artificiality and senile flunkeyism.

"In connection with Scottish song, I cannot help alluding to a notion only too current among people who believe in accomplishments and talk of culture—viz, the notion that the Scottish language is vulgar and destined to die. Nothing could be a greater mistake. If it be allowed to die it will be from the neglect of those whose first duty it was to attend to its culture; and, so far from being vulgar, it requires very little either of a cultivated ear, or of comparative philology, to know that it is, in fact, the most melodious and the most classical dialect of our common English tongue, and ought to be specially studied in all British schools, English as well as Scotch, exactly as the Athenian Greeks maintained the Doric of Ephicharnus and Pindar in the choral parts of their tragedies.

"Wishing you all the success that your patriotic exertions deserve."

The second occasion on which I met the learned Professor was somewhere in Kincardineshire, when I was touring with a small party of my own. Manson, who would be about thirteen years of age at the time, was included as a dancer. I cannot at the moment recall where the concert took place, but I remember that it came as a pleasant surprise to learn that the great Professor was in the audience.

Blackie was human to the core, and knew how to enjoy himself. That night he was in great spirits, and called out for "a guid auld Strathspey an' reel." For his special pleasure I played *Tullochgorum* and *The East Neuk o' Fife*, with variations. The Professor listened like one in a dream, and as for me, it was inspiring to play to one who was drinking in my every note.

Afterwards the Professor expressed his pleasure and appreciation in a humorous speech. He heartily congratulated Manson on his dancing, and presented him with a book of his own poems, inscribed—"From a lover of good boys—John S Blackie," with the pawky remark—"There's nae muckle hairm o' a guid Scotch reel."

At the end of the performance, Mr M'Combie Smith, who was also present, and I had a long walk with the Professor, who expressed the hope that it wouldn't be the last time he would enjoy our company, and hear "Auld Scotland's music played wi' sic virr."

"I'm shair," he added, "ye've set the heather on fire wi yer fiddle, for a'body was at the concert."

"Twa Governments"

The third and last time I saw the Professor was not under so auspicious circumstances. He was on a sick bed at Pitlochry, from which he was never to rise, and it was in acceptance of an invitation from him to "come an' cheer me a bit" that M'Combie Smith and I found ourselves under his roof.

On this occasion I was interested to make the acquaintance of a Miss Stuart, who was a relative of the late Dr Keith Norman Macdonald, of Skye, to whom I dedicated my *Harp and Claymore*.

After I had delighted the Professor with *Tullochgorum* and a number of my own strathspeys, which were favourites of his, I thought he was looking so well that he might be able to oblige us with one of his "Auld Scotch Sangs."

"Come, Professor," said I, "gie's a sang—ane o' yer auld favourites."

Turning to his wife, the Professor said—"Scott Skinner wid like me tae sing a sang. Whit d'ye say?"

The answer was a melancholy shake of his good wife's devoted head.

"D'ye see that, noo?" remarked the Professor with a merry twinkle in his eyes. "I'm under twa governments—petticoat domination and medical supervision, an' it's hard tae say which is the mair provokin'!" Even then the genial scholar was merging into the Valley of Shadows, but till the very last he was pert and pawky as aye.

Professor Granville Bantock, of the Birmingham and Midland School of Music, was another brilliant man who took an interest in my work, and frequently expressed his admiration of it, and urged me to further endeavours. On one occasion he wrote—

"I am pleased to know of the excellent work you are doing for Scottish music, and I appreciate the true spirit of Gaelic art that you embody in your playing and compositions. Go on and prosper!"

Many beautiful letters were also sent me by that great genius the late W S Gilbert, the collaborator with Sullivan in comic opera. An autographed copy of his *Bab Ballads* was one of his presents to me.

A "Record" Echo

A large number of my own strathspeys and others played by me, as many readers are doubtless aware, have for a number of years been available on gramophone records produced by various firms, and here, as showing what the gramophone has meant to me, I should like to quote from a letter written by an Aberdonian from Los Angeles, California, U.S.A.

"I had not heard a good strathspey played on the violin since I left Aberdeen twenty-eight years ago until a few days ago while passing through Toronto. While there I was looking for some imported bagpipe tunes for my phonograph and was lucky enough to find one of your strathspey records."

"This is the first real music I have heard in all those years, and though this is Sunday morning, that beautiful tune, *The Miller o' Hirn*, is in full blast. I have played this record over the telephone to all my Scotch friends and to more fully enjoy these fine Highland tunes I dress up in my kilt for the occasion."

"I find you have a number of other records which I will get the next time I am in Canada, which will be soon, as I am informed they are not for sale in the United States. Thanking you for all the pleasure you have given me, and wishing more power to your elbow," &c.

Even to Hong Kong my strathspey records have penetrated. From this outpost of the Empire a cheque arrived for me a few years ago, accompanied by a letter from two young Scottish exiles, who, to bring home a bit nearer to them, bought a gramophone and as many of my records as were for sale. Night after night they wound up the machine and listened to *The Bonnie Lass o' Bon Accord, The Laird o' Drumblair, The Miller o' Hirn,* &c., and so much pleasure did they derive from these that they decided they must send some small token of thanks and appreciation to their composer. I was instructed to buy smokes with the money enclosed, and when I tell you that it kept me in tobacco for six months—and I was an inordinately heavy smoker—you will see that the token wasn't so very small.

In a subsequent chapter I intend telling you the more interesting stories of how I composed some of my most popular pieces, but here, in the meantime, I will write of what was one of the proudest moments of my life.

A Proud Moment

This was during the last Edinburgh Exhibition, when, under the brilliant baton of Mr Faulds, the band of the 2nd Seaforth Highlanders played a selection comprising eighteen of my best airs. The rendering of them was vociferously encored by the large crowd who had listened, and surely no-one will count me conceited when I say that I thrilled with pride and pleasure when I was bidden up to the conductor's desk, there to bow my acknowledgements to the throng.

This triumph was repeated when the same band appeared in Glasgow, and again the composer had to acknowledge the plaudits of the crowd.

The Mill o' Hirn, which is the subject of a rousing strathspey by Scott Skinner.

My introduction to the Glasgow Society of Musicians, thanks to my friend , Mr J.W.Briggs, the violin expert, is also recalled with a certain feeling of pride. Dr Cowan, the conductor of the Scottish Orchestra, who recently retired from this post, was present, and it is no exaggeration to say that he was simply amazed at my interpretation of Scottish music. It was a new experience, and, in fact, a revelation to him.

No sooner had I finished playing than he led Mr Briggs and me to a side room, where he congratulated me as heartily as ever I was congratulated in my life, declaring that he had never before heard Scottish music interpreted as I had expressed it that night.

Like other violinists of any ability or eminence, I am frequently asked for the history of my fiddle. It is an Andrea Guarnarius, with the label 1690. It came into my possession in 1873, as a gift from the late Mr William Grant, of Elchies, Carron. It had probably lain in a store-room there for a century before it was found and given to me.

Mr Grant knew of the existence of the fiddle, but all his efforts to locate it in the house failed. I was in Carron in 1873 teaching about thirty little girls to dance, Mr Grant generously paying all expenses. He and I were fast friends.

The Fiddle Found

One night when I was having tea at his house he turned to me and said—"Scott Skinner, I have a fiddle somewhere in the house. I cannot find it, but I know it is here. It has been in our family for—I don't know how long. I would like to give it to you if it can be found, so we'll have another try," and with that he called for Barron, his coachman.

"You might have another look for that fiddle," said he to the coachman. "Look through all the outhouses or stores about the place."

"But I've looked before, and it cannot be found," protested Barron.

"Look again," ordered his master. "The fiddle must be somewhere about the house."

The coachman turned to go, but Mr Grant, who seemed to have a sudden inspiration, called him back. "Barron," he said, "there's a gun-case in the store-room, and it might be there."

Barron did as he was told, and luckily for me, the fiddle, after many futile searches, was found where Mr Grant imagined it might be. As was to be expected, the instrument—a Cremona—was not in the best condition after being stowed away for all those years. I took it at once to Mr J. W. Briggs, an exceedingly clever craftsman, who overhauled it in masterly fashion. As Mr Briggs handed it to me, I have played on it ever since.

The late Mr R Butter Malcolm, of St Leonard's, Perth, who possessed some beautiful old violins, valued my Andrea Guanarius at £250, while an Italian expert named Monti, whom I met at Blairgowrie, priced it at 300 guineas. Of course, had it been a Joseph, instead of an Andrea Guanarius, it would have fetched over £1000.

Monti was a great admirer of my work. On one occasion, when calling on the Strathspey and Reel Band in Inverness, he picked up a couple of books, and remarked—"Here's Bach and here's Scott Skinner. Personally, I prefer Scott Skinner."

Mr Rose Wood, a close friend of Mr Scott Skinner, and who is at present managing his Northern tour.

Eleven

How I Composed My Popular Strathspeys—Sources of Inspiration

I WAS ONLY SEVENTEEN YEARS OF AGE when I gained my first small success as a composer. This in round cash brought me the sum of five shillings for the publication in a musical journal, known as *The Key*, of a Highland polka I had composed.

I had dabbled in crotchets and quavers long ere this, but this success was the first encouragement I had received to pursue the chequered career of a composer. If you had seen me when the postal order for five shillings arrived, doubtless you would have laughed. A casual or disinterested observer would have concluded that I had received a legacy of thousands of pounds. But the "Strathspey King" in embryo, I have reason to believe, acted pretty much like many now famous authors on receiving their first bit of hard cash for a literary effort.

At the age of eighteen years I published *The Ettrick Vale Quadrilles*, the popularity of which is evident from the fact that they ran to four editions.

Then, as I was always a strathspey enthusiast, it occurred to me, presumptuous as it may appear to have been for a youth of my age, that I should make a bold bid to fill the sacred shoes of such great strathspey composers and exponents as Niel Gow and James Marshall.

The standard strathspeys when I was a youth were *The Marquis of Huntly's Farewell, Highland Whisky, Stirling Castle, The Brig o' Perth,*

Monymusk, Speed the Plough, The Devil Among the Tailors, &c., &c. These were always being played, and it occurred to me that here was my opportunity to compose something new and fresh, but maintaining an indissoluble link with the great past, for, as Professor Blackie shrewdly observed, "No true artist ever breaks with the past." So, while attempting to compose new strathspeys, I, at the same time, pledged myself to be a preserver of the best among the old ones.

The strathspey, let me explain, is the one distinctive form that Scottish instrumental music can claim to have evolved. Coming out of the mists of an undated past, it has all along maintained an intimate connection with the artistic and social life of the people, nor is its virility yet exhausted.

Strathspey's Antiquity

The origin of the strathspey cannot now be traced. The name and product are practically all that remain to guide us in any inquiry as to its historical beginnings. The name "Strathspey" argues a local, Celtic origin. Published collections of strathspeys and reels did not begin to appear until after the middle of the eighteenth century, by which time tunes like *Tullochgorum* and *The Reel o' Tulloch* were already reckoned old.

Tullochgorum, I might add, might have been entirely lost and forgotten but for the timely action of the Rev John Skinner in writing words for its rugged music.

The earliest composers of the violin strathspey (the strathspey reel had originally been a bagpipe tune) flourished during the latter half of the eighteenth century. Among these are Niel Gow and his son, Nathaniel, Donald Gow, William Marshall, Alexander M'Glashan, Robert MacIntosh, and Robert Petrie. The most imposing figure of those days is Niel Gow. His dominating personality has taken a great and permanent hold of the Scottish imagination, although his own son, Nathaniel, and William Marshall are both now reckoned above him.

Burns, who had a most intimate knowledge of national music, pronounced Marshall "the first composer of strathspeys of the age." The *Marquis of Huntly's Farewell* stands an enduring monument to his genius.

It is the custom of some superior musicians to despise and even scoff at the strathspeys as a very poor and rude kind of music, and not worth the attention of the cultivated player. The strathspey, let me admit right away, does not profess to be a highly developed form. In the realm of music it is a dialect, not a language. Yet it has its place and function. Its area may be limited, its programme humble, yet within that area and with that programme it may achieve a distinction—a perfection all its own.

But to return to my own work as a composer of strathspeys, the compositions that first brought me prominently before the public and gained me the plaudits of the people, if not all the critics, were *The Bonnie Lass o' Bon Accord* and *The Cradle Song*, which are reckoned by many able judges to be two of the finest things I have ever written. As some readers may be aware, the latter composition is now played as a church voluntary.

Then I struck out on pipe tunes, and *The Miller o' Hirn* was my first big hit on these lines, and to-day I believe I have more popular tunes for the bagpipes than any other composer, either living or dead.

Living Tunes

I have no intention of wearying my readers with the details of my life's output of original music, which, frankly speaking, has been colossal. I know that not all of it will live, but I hope, in fact I believe, that a goodly number of my melodies have entered into the social and recreative life of the people, and will live long after their composer has "shuffled off this mortal coil" and ceased to create either gems or "pot-boilers."

What will be really interesting to readers will, I believe, be a narration of the circumstances or the source of inspiration which prompted me to put some of my most popular pieces on paper.

In the first place, I should like to disillusion those who harbour a belief that I, or any creative artist for that matter, can churn out "things of beauty and a joy forever" by order or request or pump-handle methods!

A photo of the Miller o' Hirn, whose name Scott Skinner has woven into one of his greatest strathspeys.

The composer, like the poet, is born and not manufactured, although his moulding may be completed in the great foundry of life. There were times in my career when it would have been as difficult for me to compose a line of music as it would have been for a midge to survive in a snow-storm. At other times, I have felt like a Mount Vesuvius of inspiration, and melodies have poured from me like the lava from that volcano. There seemed to be no volition on my part. The thing just seemed to happen!

Some of my tunes have been composed under what might be described as very unorthodox conditions. Inspiration generally came upon me like a whirlwind, and if I had always waited until I could lay hands on beautiful white paper, all lined and ready for the notes, I know I should have composed neither as well nor as much as I have done. On more than one occasion my publishers have received a tune delivered hot from my brain or soul, just as I dashed it off on the white interior of an empty cigarette box which I have picked up from the fire-grate!

One of my best friends and benefactors was the late Mr William M'Hardy of Drumblair, who made a fortune of £100,000 in engineering enterprises in South America, and, this accomplished, he returned to his native land and lived at Forgue, near Huntly, and once every year until he died I enjoyed his hospitality there.

Soap Paper Sequel

Returned from one of these holidays, I lay in bed one night reflecting on all the kindnesses of this friend, when suddenly a tune, "pat" and complete, flashed into my head in his honour and extolation. I jumped out of bed, and my wife had to do likewise. (That is one of the disadvantages a woman incurs in marrying a man with an artistic temperament!)

"I want some paper—quick!" I called to my wife.

"Ye've used the last o' yer scored paper, Jimmie," said she. "There's nae a sheet in the hale hoose."

"Get something afore I lose this tune," I cried excitedly.

A rapid search, during which I kept humming over the tune so that it wouldn't elude me, produced nothing better than a sheet of soap paper, and on this I promptly dashed off *The Laird o' Drumblair*, much to my joy and the relief of my wife, who was able to return to bed.

Next morning I told my wife I was going to send the tune I had composed to the Laird of Drumblair. I prepared to place the original copy in an envelope for posting.

"Ye're no' gaun tae send that awfy-like paper tae the Laird," said she. "He'll jist licht his pipe wi' it!"

"Nae fear," I replied. "I'm sen'in it as it is. If a bit o' gless wis guid eneuch for Robbie Burns, a guid bit soap paper's shairly guid eneuch for me!"

And so the tune was despatched, as it had been written. The following Christmas morning a letter arrived from the Laird thanking me for the tune and accompanied by a cheque.

My wife (as wives have a habit of doing!) opened the letter for me, and handed me the contents with the remark—"Here's five guineas for yer soap paper, Jimmie!"

And each Christmas after that, during the remaining fifteen years that Mr M'Hardy lived, a cheque for a similar amount arrived, as an expression of his thanks for the tune, so it will be seen that, although written on soap paper, the melody was not quite an unsubstantial "bubble."

On one occasion I was on my way in the train from Aberdeen to Forfar. In the same compartment sat a lady with two little girls. Near Stonehaven a glimpse of "a bonnie thackit hoosie" by the side of the railroad inspired me to put a lilt on the back of an old envelope.

Table-Cloth "Scored"

A North-bound goods train passed as I finished the melody. Just then one of the little girls exclaimed—"Oh, what's that?" I presumed she was referring to what I had been writing, and I politely replied—"Oh, it's a good s-train." The little girl, however, had referred to the passing train, but my reply, it dawned on me suddenly, had been quite suitable, although the pun was unconsciously perpetrated.

Whilst on tour with Mr George Walker I made quite a host of tunes. One of these was in honour of George, who, as I said before, was a true friend to me.

We were dining in our lodgings at Kirkcaldy, when one of the party said to me—"If you think so much of Geordie Walker, why have you never made a tune about him?"

By a strange coincidence my own thoughts had been running in this very direction all that day, and when thus remonstrated with, I found the tune I had been evolving was complete and "pat" in my head.

"I will sune dae that," I replied. "Gi'e me a bit of paper."

Nobody, I remember, could oblige at the moment, and someone went to see if the landlady could help me out. In the meantime, however, the tune so insistently clamoured for expression that, yielding to impulse, I started to score it off on the landlady's table-cloth, and by the time that the paper-seeking individual had returned from a successful search, the tune of Geordie Walker had been born on fine linen, if not on purple!

The "purple," when I resumed a normal view of things, I apprehended, would be evident in the landlady's face when she beheld her tablecloth!

"I hope the landlady won't see this," I remarked apprehensively.

"Oh, never mind that," said Mr Walker, who was delighted with the tune. And then, to further complicate matters, he cut the piece of linen containing the tune clean out of the cloth.

Beholding my woe-begone expression, Mr Walker assured me it was all right, and later I know he did make matters right with the landlady. Perhaps he has the lacerated tablecloth to this day.

The tune was then transferred to paper, and that night the audience in the Adam Smith Hall, Kirkcaldy, had the honour of hearing its first public rendering.

A Winsome Widow

Time and place made very little difference to me when I was in the mood for composing. For instance, I arrived at the Muir of Ord to give a concert, and put up at the hotel at Tarradale, the proprietrix of which turned out to be a very old friend of mine, a widow named Mrs MacDonald. I had met her first when I was a dancing master in Elgin. I was pleasantly surprised to find her running the hotel, and she, in turn, was absolutely delighted to meet me and talk over old times.

The concert was on the Saturday night, and we remained over Sunday in the hotel. A number of Americans who were in the district for fishing were included among the guests. Our hostess took a great delight in explaining to the Yankees who I was and what I had done, was doing, &c. Then at luncheon she suddenly remarked—"It's a funny thing that Mr Scott Skinner, who professes to think so much of me, never wrote a tune for me!"

I reflected a minute or two, and then, feeling that inspiration was coming, I begged to be excused from the table, and retired to my bedroom, promising I should return in a minute or so.

The concert part at present touring the North. Left to right—Miss Cathie Macdonald, dancer; Mr Harvey Hamilton, tenor; Miss Jean Wilson Brown, contralto; Mr J. Ross Wood, manager; Mr Scott Skinner; Miss Olga Ironside, soprano; and Miss Mabel Desmond, pianist.

By the time I reached my bedroom the tune was a complete conception, and it was a very simple matter to trace it on to paper.

I returned to the luncheon room, and placed the manuscript, without a title, on the mantlepiece. Then I took up my violin and played it over a few times, and later got one of the American guests to accompany me on the piano.

On all hands it was agreed that I had composed a "ripping good tune," and, amid the congratulations I was receiving, I turned to Mrs MacDonald—"You cannot now complain that I haven't made a tune to you, for I make you a present of this one, and I will call it *The Rose o' Tarradale.*"

The widow was flabbergasted, but recovering her breath, expressed her thanks as well as she could. "Well, Mr Scott Skinner," said she, "it's one of the sweetest tunes I ever heard."

"But not half so sweet as you are!" I replied with gallantry, and I meant it, for she was a sweet woman in every way. It was chiefly due to her unflagging efforts on our behalf that we enjoyed a "bumper" house at our concert the previous night.

Somewhat similar were the circumstances under which I composed the tune *Violet Davidson*, which is to the honour of the good lady of the Aberdeen Beach Pavilion.

A Promise Kept

I was a frequent visitor at the house of Mr and Mrs Thomson during my touring days, Mr George Walker generally accompanying me. On one occasion after tea Violet turned to Mr Walker and said—"I hear that Mr Skinner has made a tune for you. Let me tell you, it's a long time since he promised to write one for me, but I'm still waiting for him to keep his promise."

Thus reminded of my unfulfilled promise I felt a little ashamed of myself, for Violet and I were always the best of friends. I therefore resolved to implement the promise on the spot if it were at all possible.

I sat for a long time cogitating, but inspiration is a thing that cannot be forced. That night it refused to come! All the while I sat thinking the others continued talking, and I guess I must have given some stupid answers to the questions addressed to me. I was not one of them for the time being; I was living on the stilts of abstraction.

I had decided, however, that it was a futile quest, and had come down from my poetical perch when a chance remark by Mr George Walker gave me the cue I was needing, and urged me to pencil and paper forthwith, to indite the hornpipe and reel now known as *Violet Davidson*.

I must admit that the germ of the idea came from Mr Walker, who is himself, by the way, no mean composer. This tune, with which Mrs Thomson was delighted, I played two nights later at Laurencekirk in order to see how it would "take." So great was the reception accorded my playing of it that I telegraphed Violet—"Your tune a terrific success; having it published at once."

In a letter of grateful acknowledgement, Violet said she was proud to be included among the many famous men and women to whom I had dedicated my compositions.

One of the most popular tunes ever I wrote, and one which is still in great demand when I appear on the platform, is *Our Highland Queen*, dedicated to her late Majesty Queen Victoria. My frequent visits to Balmoral Castle and its lovely environs and the interest the old Queen took in me when I was pushing my way as a dancing master prompted me to the theme.

Our Highland Queen

When I had written this tune, which pleased me better than anything else I ever wrote (I don't know why!), I took it to the late Bob Grant, of Peterhead, with a request that he should write words for it. Bob was a poet of no mean order, but I remember he had a quaint and original method of assimilating the lilt of a tune before setting to work. This was to note on a piece of paper by means of dots and dashes (like the Morse code) the accented syllables of each line as I played the tune over to him on the fiddle. One of his verses for *Our Highland Queen* reads—

> *The bluebell may forget to spring,*
> *The Gelder cease to flow;*
> *But Deeside men can ne'er forget*
> *The loyalty they owe.*

I then took the score and words to an Aberdeen firm of lithographers and had these lithographed on white satin, and despatched the completed article to Balmoral as a present to Her Majesty. This she graciously acknowledged by the hand of Lieut-General Sir Henry Ponsonby, K.C.B.

This white white satin souvenir, I was subsequently informed, was, by command of the Queen, incorporated in a fire-screen at Balmoral, and it is possible it is there to this day.

The scene of the *Weeping Birches of Kilmorack*, which is the theme of another of my melodies, is on the river Beauly in the Dhriem Pass. The river here runs through a deep gorge. The environment is rugged and romantic. The birches growing on the river banks are very pretty, and the whole scene is well worth the brush of a painter.

It was while I was the guest of Mr Donald Morison, of Beauly, that I had the pleasure of viewing this sylvan spot. We drove to it, Dr MacDonald, of the same ilk, accompanying us. Some time prior to this visit there had been an accident at the spot. A traction engine with a couple of trucks fell from the road, a distance of 100 feet, into the gorge, causing the death of two men. A strange phenomenon was observed after the accident, when most of the birches within thirty yards of the scene of the accident began to wither away. When I saw them they stood leafless and forlorn-looking and covered with fungi.

The pathos of the story deeply appealed to me, and that night the tune of the *Weeping Birches of Kilmorack* literally poured from my soul on to paper. I was obsessed by the tragic story, and had to give it expression.

Twelve

More Stories of My Strathspeys—The Bonnie Lass o' Bon Accord

IF I WERE ASKED TO STATE WHICH of my melodies I consider to be the most popular, I should unhesitatingly reply, *The Bonnie Lass o' Bon Accord.* It has had a wonderful vogue, and, curiously enough, the story connected with its composition is, I believe, the most interesting relating to my strathspeys.

Its inspirer was a young girl named Wilhelmina Bell (now a married woman with six of a family, residing in Aberdeen). In December 1884 I was holding dancing classes in the Silver Street Hall, Aberdeen.

One evening I and some friends were invited to a house in Union Terrace. There I found a girl performing the menial task of a servant, who, it was plain to see, was a "cut" above the ordinary servant lass of those days. I was both interested and surprised, and my surprise was heightened when the floor was cleared for dancing, for Wilhelmina proved herself a splendid "tripper of the light fantastic toe."

At the very first opportunity I got into conversation with her, and when the girl told me that her father used to play bass fiddle for my father, the way was paved for further confidences.

"You're a splendid dancer," I said. "Hoo comes it that you are a servant lass here?"

The girl's eyes filled with tears as she made reply—"My father," said she, "was a farmer up Deeside at Cockley, but he's living oot at Newtonhill now."

"Hoo's that?" I asked sympathetically, sensing tragedy.

"Oh," sobbed the lass, "my father signed a bill for a freen', an' got it a' tae pey. That was his ruin. He is now glad of a day's work, and that is why I am here."

"Never mind, my lassie," said I cheerfully, clapping her on the shoulders, "I'll mak' a tune that'll maybe keep ye in min' when we're baith deid."

Next morning under the same roof I composed *The Bonnie Lass o' Bon Accord.*

The Landlady's Warning

When I was engrossed in its composition two ladies called to see me. My hostess, knowing what I was about, refused to let them in to see me, remarking—"I canna let ye in noo, for ye micht get the ink bottle in your face, because he's writin' a new tune!"

That afternoon I went out with the tune in my pocket. Meeting Mr Alexander Dinnie, an Aberdeen photographer I knew well, I showed the score to him.

"Man," he exclaimed, "there's something great in that tune. Ye'll need to mak' it something aboot Bon Accord" (Aberdeen).

Just at that moment who should pass but Wilhelmina herself, bent on an errand.

"There," I whispered to Dinnie, "goes the bonnie lass the tune's about!"

A view of Forres, where Mr Scott Skinner wrote his famous "Cradle Song."

99

"I've got it!" exclaimed Dinnie. "Ca' it *The Bonnie Lass o' Bon Accord*," and I did.

When I was teaching dancing at Forres some 40 years ago, I engaged a room in the local hotel for the purpose. One night I remember I went into the wrong room by mistake, and pausing at the threshold, beheld a touching sight. One of the most beautiful women I had ever seen was bending over the cradle of a sick child. I backed out very quietly, but that glimpse I had of the interior of that room, charged, as it was, with sentiment and poetry, gave me the theme for a great melody.

Here, I soliloquised, was a beautiful lady, watching night and day over her little son, who was the heir to a title and large estates. The lady was probably a widow, and if the boy died, &c., &c. Thus I romanced and ruminated, and *The Cradle Song*, which is played in churches as a voluntary, was born.

Verses, written for this tune by Mr Alexander Hastings, Huntly, are very appropriate. Here are four of them—

> *Spirits that guard young children,*
> *Enter here to-night,*
> *O'er my fevered darling,*
> *Watch till morning light.*
>
> *From our home for ever*
> *Went my love away,*
> *Crossed the darkling river,*
> *Entered endless day.*
>
> *Sleep, my own fair darling,*
> *I will cling to thee,*
> *Sure my cup of sorrow*
> *Cannot fuller be.*
>
> *Oh! my life is lonely,*
> *Oft my thoughts are wild;*
> *Ah, my heart were broken*
> *Did I lose my child.*

Something Satanic

It was also in Forres that the famous *Deil's Concert* was formulated.

One night an irresistible impulse to compose something "Satanic" took hold of me, and the tune which subsequently appeared in my Logie

Collection under the name of *The Rover* was the sequel. The original idea of the composition was that I had descended to Hades, and there held converse with His Majesty of the Tail and Cloven Hoof. Along these lines was built up a poem known as *The Deil's Concert*, from which I shall quote presently.

When I had evolved the tune, my next thought was as to who was to write verses for it. My first choice was the late Mr William Martin, who was a schoolmaster at Inverkeithnie. I wanted words to suit a sort of demon melody, something seething with fire and brimstone, I told him, and set him the pace in a few lines written by myself, which read—

> *The deil had a concert in hell ae nicht, an' I was invited there.*
> *Of coorse, I did gang, be it richt, be it wrang, for fiddlers maun*
> *   gang ilka where;*
> *Th' flair o't wis causied (causewayed) wi' hypocrites' skulls, an'*
> *   th' faur end wis as dark as jet,*
> *An' those that I never expeckit tae meet were th' very first folk*
> *   that I met.*
> *Nae winner I shook at th' brimstane an' brook an' at hell's blood-*
> *   curdling roar*
> *As forward I strode whaur th' blue lowe showed frae the bolted*
> *   infernal ha' door.*

At this point verses written by Mr George Ingram (who wrote under the pen-name "Gramin," and is now resident in the United States) were inserted. I quote the following—

> *Auld Cloutie looked ower wi' a satisfied glower when he saw me*
> *   gang stotterin' ben,*
> *Says he, "Jimmie, man, come gie me yer han', ye're welcome tae*
> *   Horny's fire-en,'*
> *I've lang watched wi' interest yer onward career, I've rejoiced at*
> *   yer ilka success.*
> *But I like ye ower devotedly tae wish yer presence here for*
> *   onything beyond a social gless;*
> *Yer fiddlers an' yer poets come a' doon here tae see me, but I*
> *   widna tak' them in,*
> *For I tell them very plainly, for I always speak humanely, they*
> *   canna work here—there's sic a din!"*

Hospitality having been dispensed in the "lower regions," with evil spirits "wi' blue lichts in their bunnets," as waiters, and the Deil having enjoyed a siesta, I am commanded to play a tune. The tale is taken up by Mr William Martin—

> *My fiddle I strung, and its chords, as they rung, set their black,*
> *   blistered shanks a-stirrin'.*
> *But, O! what a yell resounded through Hell when I struck up*
> *   The Miller o' Hirn,*

Wi' hooch an' halloo, through th' figure they flew, wi' their
    thumbs snappin' fire like th' flint,
An' like kye in th' bis or like snakes when they hiss, their lang
    tails swung curlin' ahint.

Auld Satin arose from his deep, drunken doze, an' rubbin' his red
    e'en, he swore,
"Ye're a gey clever chiel, nae man yet nor deil, played a fiddle sae
    finely afore;
And if when ye're dune wi' th' sun an' th' moon, ye come doon my
    lang, reekin' lum,
There's a welcome haunshake for guid fellowship's sake awaiting
    ye here when ye come.
Whit treatment ye'll hae I canna jist say, for the fiddlers sent here
    are but few,
But there's ae place in Hell whaur there bubbles a well, an' I'll
    keep that cool corner for you."

The Auld Mill

The tune *The Miller o' Hirn*, referred to above, was amongst my early efforts, but, according to competent judges, it is one of my very best. The old miller of Hirn, John Johnston by name, and my grandfather were married to sisters, and as a boy both the miller and the mill were objects of great veneration to me. Many a visit I paid to the mill, and later in life the feelings it had generated returned clamouring for expression on the lined sheet.

The inspiration, I remember, came upon me suddenly when I was in Banchory, and I rushed into the home of my good friends the M'Ewans, calling out to Miss Isobel—"Isobel, Isobel, there's a tune bizzin' in my head—come quick!" I scored the melody on paper, and Miss Isobel played it over on the piano and pronounced it "Splendid," and that was how *The Miller o' Hirn* was created or re-created.

In this tune, which has been heard in almost every quarter of the globe, I have faithfully produced the effect of the water running down the mill lade on to the wheel.

My strathspey, *Hector Macdonald*, which is to the memory of Scotland's most famous soldier, was composed at Monikie on receipt of the news of his tragic death in Paris. My second wife brought up the report of the grim happening when I was in bed one morning, and so grieved and shocked was I that I rose and dressed, and in the most melancholy fame of mind made my way downstairs. Without speaking a word to my wife, I took up a pencil and commenced to write, and the lilt, which was already complete in my brain, fell unintermittingly on to paper. The very same day the original copy, without correction, went to my printers in Edinburgh, and the tune is still preserved in its original form.

The story of how I made the tune known as *The President* and how it came to be rechristened by that name may also be interesting. A few years prior to my American tour, when Manson, Madame de Langlee, and I were living in the new hotel at Ellon Station, I began one day on one of the hotel sheets of notepaper to throw off a melody which seemed to me trivial, yet full of intricacies. It was a sort of "Carnival de Venice" arrangement.

The President

It was a long time before I knew myself what I was aiming at. The eccentricities of the German Emperor (fads with a grim purpose, we now know to our cost) in ordering his troops out at night, &c., were very much in mind when I was writing, and the melody was really a reflection of the Kaiser's ongoings, so the tune came to be known as *The Emperor*.

When I was in the artistes' room at the Lennox Lyceum, New York, Jamie Blaikie, the accompanist, shouted, "Your turn, 'King'," and I asked, "What am I down for?"

"*The President,*" was the reply.

"You've surely made a mistake, Jamie," said I; "you must mean *The Emperor.*"

"Get away with you," was Jamie's smiling rejoinder; "there's no Emperors here—it's all Presidents."

I made no demur. I realised I was being helped by a master tactician! And the tune in question has remained *The President* to this day.

Mention of the American tour reminds me that *The Fallen Chief* was penned to the memory of Piper Willie MacLennan, but you already know the tragic story that I have epitomised in this melody.

Before I take leave of my indulgent readers, I should like to make a few remarks about what various ill-informed and caustic critics have said about my work from time to time.

The great work of my life has been composing music for the people of Scotland. I have not composed symphonies for a full orchestra, nor set to music a play or poem with orchestral accompaniment, to be produced with a great flourish of trumpets before musical dilettanti, and played or sung once or twice a year, and now and again at intervals of several years or never again. These are the kinds of music to compose if one wants to make a noise in the musical world, but they are not of the kind that reaches the hearts of the people.

The True Test

The music that reaches and lives in the hearts of the people is the music that they whistle or sing at their daily toil or in their hours of recreation, that the mother croons o'er the cradle, and that accompanies her children, a joyous companion, through life. Music thus entering into the hearts of the people proves by this test its real worth.

A song or air or any piece of music may be faultlessly sung or played by the best singers or musicians, it may be rapturously applauded by the most fashionable audiences, pronounced first-class by the leading critics, and yet soon sink into oblivion.

Thousands of songs and pieces of music have been faultlessly sung and played, loudly applauded, and favourably criticised within the past hundred years that are to-day lying dead and forgotten.

Many of the finest songs of Robert Burns were first sung by Kirsty Flint, wife of a Dumfriesshire mason, over a hundred years ago, in a lowly cottage to a single hearer, who was both audience and critic of melodies by composers whose very names in many instances are now unknown.

Are these songs and their melodies, so unostentatiously launched on the sea of time, dead and forgotten? The songs first sung in the lowly cottage by the mason's wife to one Dumfriesshire farmer have gone to the uttermost ends of the earth, and are now sung by thousands to audiences of millions.

By the same test I am bold enough to hope that many of my airs will live, circulate among, and permeate the life of the people. My *Miller o' Hirn* strathspey was not long published until it became a street classic, while *The Bonnie Lass o' Bon Accord* became popular almost in the twinkling of an eye. Both these tunes, not to mention others, I claim without boastfulness, have made their way into the hearts of the Scottish people, and, I believe, will remain there when I am no more.

Some of you may ask if my reputation rests on two airs, and I would reply—By no means, but even if it did, I maintain it is a highly creditable performance to have written one song or composed one melody that is destined to live.

My Best Work

I have frequently been asked to name my best composition and a few others in the order of merit, but it's a job I never felt inclined to undertake. So eminent a judge as the late Dr Keith Norman MacDonald, editor of *The Skye Collection*, thought that my best strathspeys in order of merit are the *Brig o' Potarch*, *Miller's Rant*, *Glenlivet*, and *The Miller o' Hirn*.

One lady judge considered *The Miller o' Hirn* not only my best strathspey, but (excuse the seeming egotism) the best of all strathspeys.

At various times I have been charged with gross plagiarism. For instance, when *The Bonnie Lass o' Bon Accord* became a popular favourite, it was subjected to criticism of various kinds. Attention was drawn to the fact that the first six notes, or, including two grace notes, the first eight notes of it, are the same as the first eight notes of Nathaniel Gow's *Miss Graham of Inchbrakie*. What of that, say I. The melodies as a whole are totally dissimilar after the opening notes. A tune may be to all intents and purposes strictly original, and yet contain several consecutive notes exactly the same as are found in another tune.

If anyone will examine, not the first six or eight, but the first fourteen, notes of *Auld Lang Syne* and *My Heart is Sair for Somebody* it will be found that, except the third and fourth notes, the other twelve are identical.

Compare also the first parts of *Rory o' More* and *Monymusk*. In Marshall's most famous strathspey, *The Marquis of Huntly's Farewell*, of the first eleven notes all, except the second and third, are identical with the first eleven of the *Braes o' Auchtertyre*.

I could multiply such instances indefinitely, but I have written enough to show that, if the sticklers for originality object to the *Miller o' Hirn* and *The Bonnie Lass o' Bon Accord* because one contains a bar and the other part of a bar, in which the notes are the same as in other airs, they must, to be consistent, object with even greater emphasis to many of the finest songs by Burns and to many of the finest airs by the best and most famous composers of the past and present.

A Tribute

That my work has the true Scottish ring is my sincere claim. It may be epitomised in the words of William Aitken, the poet—

> *The reek o' the cot in the clachan,*
> *The burnie that rins past the door,*
> *The red-cheekit lassie aye lauchin'*
> *While herdin' the kye on the moor.*

Having thus disposed of the destructive breed known as critics, I should like, ere closing this rather rambling narrative of my career, to quote from a eulogistic poem by Mr W D Jeffrey, Rhynie, expressing the hope that it is typical of the service I have performed for all who have listened to my compositions—

I had a nicht, an' only ane,
  Wi' James Scott Skinner,
Nae long ago in Aberdeen.
  Wi' James Scott Skinner.
An' sic a nicht I never saw,
  Nor spent afore wi' great or sma',
For I could hardly win awa'
  Frae James Scott Skinner.

The happy soul-inspiring strains
  O' James Scott Skinner
Gart a' my bluid dance in my veins
  Wi' James Scott Skinner.
For never yet heard I sic play
  In a' my life, I'm safe to say;
The Paganini of the day
  Is James Scott Skinner.

"Wi' hornpipes, jigs, strathspeys, an' reels,"
  Frae James Scott Skinner,
Time flew as gin't had been on wheels,
  Wi' James Scott Skinner.
Whiles Bonnie Lass *an'* Highland Queen,
  Sweet Gairloch *an' the* Earl o' Deane,
The verra tears brocht tae my een,
  Wi' James Scott Skinner.

Oor fiddlers a' maun sit in rear
  O' James Scott Skinner.
For we the like had never here
  O' James Scott Skinner.
Nor was there ever ane, I trew,
  Save Paganini or Niel Gow,
Could wield the sprightly fiddle bow
  Like James Scott Skinner.

Long may the elbow joint yet jink
  O' James Scott Skinner.
For few can gaur the measure clink
  Like James Scott Skinner.
An' when at last he's ta'en awa',
  On Manson may his mantle fa',
Wha may as guid a bow yet draw
  As James Scott Skinner.

The poet expresses the hope that my mantle will fall on my son. That happiness, as I indicated in a previous chapter, is denied me in the winter of my days; but other joys, appreciated all the more for their belatedness, have come to cheer my "auld he'rt."

And now a final word ere I part with *People's Journal* readers. It has yielded me wondrous satisfaction to pen these memories of a chequered career—a life full of ups and downs, joys and sorrows, failures and successes. If it has given the readers of the dear old "P.J." as much pleasure to read these reminiscences of a fiddler as it has given the fiddler to write them I am supremely happy.

Life's voyage for me has oft been tempestuous. There were times when the waves of adversity almost overwhelmed me, but happily I survived, and at last I have dropped anchor in a harbour of peace and happiness. That harbour, I am proud to know, is in the hearts of the Scottish people.

SCOTT SKINNER CONCERTS.

ST. ANDREW'S HALL, BANFF

MONDAY, 8th JULY,

AT 8 O'CLOCK.

A NICHT WI'

SCOTT SKINNER

SCOTLAND'S GREATEST VIOLINIST.

Scott Skinner is acknowledged by Press and Public, without exception, to be the living embodiment of our national music. Not only as an exponent on the violin, but as a composer, he stands unrivalled. He is the Paganini of Scotch music.

During his American tour, hundreds travelled miles to hear him. Never miss an opportunity of hearing our national melodies PLAYED, as they can only be by one man—SCOTT SKINNER.

DOVE PATERSON,

Elocutionist, in his inimitable Recitations.

DANCE ARTIST,

Master Manson Scott Skinner,

The most Graceful Juvenile Dancer in Scotland.

Professor Scott, Elocutionist,

In his famous Characteristic Scotch Selections, including his Side-splitting "Sowda Water," "John and Tibbie's Dispute," "Legend of St. Swithin," &c.

ADMISSION---6d, 1s, and 1s 6d.

W. MILLER, GENERAL PRINTER, 16 DEVERON STREET, HUNTLY.

108

Appendix

❋ SCOTT SKINNER CONCERTS. ❋

Will visit this Town shortly.

CROWDED HOUSES NIGHTLY.

☞ Don't neglect hearing Scotland's Greatest
Violinist.

*Mr Scott Skinner will perform several Fav-
ourite Selections on the Violin, including "The
President," (composed specially for his recent
American tour, and received everywhere with
unbounded applause). Also, "Hielan' Donald,"
with Variations, and "East Neuk o' Fife" with
Variations. Come and listen to "Tullochgorum,"
but keep your feet at rest, and when you leave
the hall you will say that*

The happiest hour that e'er ye spent,
Was spent wi' Skinner's fiddle O.'

Master Manson Scott Skinner,
Champion Juvenile Dancer of Scotland,
will perform the "Lonach Highland Fling," "Seann
Truibbhs," "Scarf Dance," "Sand Dance," etc.
*A better Exhibition of graceful Dancing it is
difficult to conceive.*

❋PROFESSOR SCOTT,❋

*will give some of his Recitations. Come and hear
him recite in the good old Doric. Everybody should
hear "Sowda Water," "Waesome Carl," and
"Speed Onward." Encored every performance.*

ADMISSION===6d, 1s, and 1s 6d.

W. MILLER, PRINTER, DEVERON STREET, HUNTLY.

110

Scott Skinner's "Great Time" in America

Driven Through Boston
in Gold and White Chariot

THE "STRATHSPEY KING" has returned to his native Deeside after a sojourn of some nine weeks in the land of the almighty dollar, and, although he failed in his quest for the fiddling championship cup of the world he is richer in experience and in that wealth, that is beyond all price—physical and mental health.

"I've had a great time," he said to me when I saw him "but 'east - west, hame's best,' and I'm glad to be back in dear old Aberdeen."

The feeling I am sure is reciprocated. We are all delighted to see our "grand old man" amongst us again, cheery and bright as ever, his compactly built figure, garbed in kilt and shod in buckled sheen, restores Union Street, his favourite promenade to its wonted glory.

Westward Ho!

In the long talk I had with him I was provided with many details of his transatlantic trip, the kindness of his hosts, and his triumphal march—for it was nothing less—through that large slice of the state of which Boston is the centre.

Scott Skinner and his secretary sailed from Liverpool on the *R.M.S. Caronia* on March 13, and reached Boston on the 21st of the same month. A first-rate sailor, whose sea legs are a natural gift, he enjoyed every hour on the voyage, and, as was to be expected, he was

lionised by his fellow passengers when it leaked out, as it did soon after the steamer cleared the Mersey, that his object in adventuring west was to capture, for puir auld Scotland the premier guerdon for competitive fiddling of reels, jigs and strathspeys. He was the choice of the Royal Society of Clans in America for the task, and, knowing the man and his reputation, who could doubt the wisdom of the selection.

The Earl of Lauderdale, in an especial degree, was intrigued by the novelty of the situation and was foremost among those who rallied round the octogenarian and saw to his entertainment and comfort. The ship orchestra also joined in the hero-worshipping, including in one of their nightly programmes a selection of the best known Scott Skinner compositions, while on another evening the "King" returned the compliment by giving the star turn—also Scottish.

But pleasant as all this was it was merely the prelude, the overture of the band, as it were, to the raising of the curtain on the real play. Things occurred in great style when the *Caronia* reached her berth in Boston Harbour. The quay was thronged with clansmen, all in full Highland costumes; beyond them was a dense pack of the general public; all around the warehouses and other buildings were beflagged; and in front, impressive in their vari-coloured array, were the massed brass and pipe bands of the various Caledonian Societies.

Among the musicians, by the way, were no fewer than four Methlick men, and brothers at that.

The Chiefs of the Royal Order of Scottish Clans, Messrs. Malcolm and Ramsay, boarded the vessel and heartily greeted the "King." The musicians sounded a magnificent fanfare, and the spectators cheered. An address of welcome was read, the lady visitor was presented with a beautiful bouquet of roses, heather intertwined, after which the couple were escorted to a white and gold motor coach in waiting, and so on to the Bellevue Hotel.

Photographers were busy at this stage. The cinema men were also active, their productions being afterwards the thrill of many of the city picture houses; but one of the best "snaps" was that secured by the Earl of Lauderdale from the quarterdeck of the *Caronia*, and which has been not inappropriately, entitled after a famous painting, *Dropping the Pilot*.

The space from the docks to the hotel was traversed mid the greatest excitement.

"They do let themselves go these American cousins of ours," Mr Scott Skinner said with a laugh; "they fairly flung themselves at me as if I was a 'King' indeed! And they do believe in flags. These were everywhere and at Bellevue Hotel simply overwhelming. I was told afterwards that in the procession the Scottish and Irish standards had been shown together for the first time in history, and that I might consider myself highly honoured, which of course I did."

Magnificent Fanfare

A gorgeous dinner was given in the evening. The company was large and representative of all the clan societies, and there Mr Scott Skinner was presented with a parchment of acknowledgement, which is only awarded to Gaels of long official standing. That an exception should be made in this case was considered as the acme of distinction—recognition could not further go.

The day following the arrival Mr Scott Skinner paid a ceremonial visit to the Governor of Boston and the principal Councillors, after which he trained to Portland, Maine, where there was a repetition of the parade, of the enthusiasm, and of the banqueting that distinguished the Boston welcome. The same evening an inter-urban car conveyed him and his party to Lewiston, where they put up at the De Witt Hotel. On their way thither, which was accomplished not without difficulty owing to the immense concourse that filled the streets, the old man was greeted in accents which left no doubt as to the nationality of those from whom they proceeded.

One old woman, in a finely-seasoned Glasgow speech, shouted "Man, Scott Skinner, ahm gled tae see ye! Are they a' fine in Aiberdeen? An' is the toon aye it wis?" The "King," one may be sure, always had his answer in kind ready.

The banquet which was held on the first evening at Lewiston, was preceded by a pretty little ceremony which may be regarded as the equivalent of our presentation of the freedom of the city—namely, that of handing to the visitor, "the stranger within the gates," the keys of the town. Mayor Wiseman delivered an ornate oration on the occasion, and Rev Dr Finnie of the Baptist Church, told stories of which it may be said that they were nearly, but not quite, as good as those manufactured in Aberdeen.

One "chestnut" however, was related which seemed to show that America after all is not exactly up-to-date. The tale related to the Oxford procession in which the role of Appius Claudius was filled by the local butcher, who, overburdened by his coat of mail and plumed helmet, took occasion of a halt by the way to remove his headgear and wipe his perspiring forehead. An inquisitive student, seeing him thus engaged, asked "Are you Appius Claudius?" to which the overheated and tired pork flesher groaned out in reply, "No, I'm as un-Appy as 'ell!" The story will be recognised as an old friend. I heard it myself many years ago, but not from a Baptist minister.

Competition a Failure

Lewiston retained the "King" for the better part of a fortnight. There it was that the "World's Fiddling Competition" took place, regarding which, although it was the magnet that drew our veteran across the seas, it is not necessary to do more than repeat briefly what has already been said about it. The time of testing was spread over a full week. Financially it was a failure, owing to the stormy weather that prevailed; and musically considered a travesty of what our hero expected it to be.

A night each was devoted to hearing the Canadian, the Irish, the American, the Scottish, the unclassified, and the final contestants, and most unfortunately for Scott Skinner, the playing of Strathspeys was banned, and only Reels and Jigs were allowed. When his turn came he started with *Birlin' Reels*, only to find that his pianoforte accompanist was on to a different tune altogether, and that when corrected he could neither keep time nor regard the rhythm.

The "King" lost his temper, brought his performance to an abrupt stop, and bowing to his mystified audience, marched off the platform. He thereby lost the championship but maintained his self-respect. Another thing that hurt

his dignity was that a jazz band had been engaged for the occasion and that contests in the playing of melodeons, mouth-organs, jews-harps, &c., were features of the entertainment.

The following Sunday Mr Scott Skinner took part in the service at Dr Finnie's Church, giving his own arrangement of *Loch Lomond* in which snatches of such gems as *Back to the Hills, The Road to the Isles,* &c., are introduced as illustrative variations that in the congregation there were present many Scotsmen and Scotswomen was evident from the furtive wiping of eyes as the strains of the plaintive hamewith melodies filled the sacred edifice.

Speeding the Parting Guest

Thereafter engagements to appear at concerts all over the country poured in. "If I had accepted all the offers that were made," Mr Scott Skinner said, "I should have remained in America for several years, but my doctor's orders were to come home before the hot season arrived, and so I had to refuse them. The only places I visited were Holyoak, Fitsburg, Pantucket (Rhode Island), Portsmouth, and two others, and when I left for home, I was again 'piped' to the steamer. The last thing I saw at Boston was a number of girls footing *Highland Laddie* on the roof of the wharf, and the last thing I heard was the blare of brass bands playing *Will ye no' Come Back Again!*"

"A kind, hospitable people are the Americans," is the old man's summing up of his unique experience, "and I shall never forget the great time they gave me 'over there'."

—People's Journal 29.5.1926

"The Strathspey King"

Passing of Mr Scott Skinner

Scottish Music's Loss

ABERDEEN AS A CITY and Scottish music have lost one of their outstanding and picturesque personalities by the death of Mr James Scott Skinner, known the world o'er as "The Strathspey King." Mr Skinner, who was in his 84th year, had never recovered from a trip which he undertook to America last year. For his years his spirit and physical vigour were wonderful, but the journey taxed his strength to an injurious degree, and for some time he had been in feeble health. He passed away at an early hour this morning at his residence, 25 Victoria Street, Aberdeen.

National Figure

"Frae Maidenkirk to John o' Groats," and across the Border and "wherever Scotsmen gather," the news will be commented upon, for "Scott Skinner," as he was familiarly known, was a national figure. Memory will conjure up a small, yet well-knit figure, clad in the garb of Old Gaul, and moving with light, springy footsteps towards the footlights, with his beloved fiddle, to charm and delight. Who that ever saw him could forget him as he strode forward and made his bow—in these later year, grey-haired, yet erect, with sparkling eyes glancing from underneath shaggy brows, looking every inch a Highland chieftain, and bringing with him, as it seemed, just that touch of romance

which at once created the atmosphere for his inimitable music. So he bore himself proudly—as an artiste, a musician; the fiddle aside, his was a genial, kindly, homely soul.

Happiest in the North

His life took him far away but he was always happiest in the north and near his native Deeside. He was born on August 5th 1843, in Banchory-Ternan. His father, William Skinner, was a gardener, but became well-known in Aberdeenshire and Kincardineshire as a teacher of dancing. Dancing and the fiddle go together, and at an early age young James learned both arts. His heart lay chiefly towards the fiddle and that was his contribution in the carrying on of dancing classes at Bucksburn - an early experience - in conjunction with his brother John Scott Skinner.

But he began his real musical life as a protege of Dr Mark, a German, who founded a school for boys at Manchester. He taught the youngsters all sorts of instruments and they toured the country as Dr Mark's Little Men. They had a command performance before Queen Victoria at Windsor Castle. In later life he played at Balmoral Castle.

Visit to U.S.

While most of his professional life was spent in Scotland, he became a familiar figure at London and the large provincial centres. About 1893 he went to America with a Scottish company led by the once well-known Piper Willie M'Lennan, Edinburgh, but the latter died in the course of the tour, which was abandoned. A year ago he recrossed the Atlantic to take part in a competition of violin players of over 70 years, but the event did not suit him, as he found that it was Irish jigs and such like which were expected, and he left the stage in high dudgeon. One can almost imagine the scene as the veteran turned away with flashing eyes! He made a number of appearances elsewhere, but, as indicated, the long journey proved too much for him.

In tours at home and abroad he was associated with the most outstanding Scottish artistes, including Sir Harry Lauder, whom he accompanied on the great comedian's early venture in London. In Scotland, of course, he was supreme, and in the north a welcome friend. Not very long ago he was welcomed with the quotation from Burns :-

> *Hale be your heart,*
> *Hale be your fiddle,*
> *Lang may your elbuck jink and diddle*
> *To cheer you thro' the weary widdle*
> *O' wardly cares.*

Live in His Music

The heart, that seemed so full of the sunshine of his music, is still, the elbuck will no longer jink and diddle over the fiddle, and the fire of his Strathspeys and reels will never again urge an audience to take the floor, but Scott Skinner will live in his music. He was a composer as well as a player, and his Strathspeys and reels will keep his memory green. He published a collection in 1868; his *Mill o' Hirn* collection appeared in 1881, the Elgin collection in 1884, the Logie collection

in 1888, and the Harp and Claymore collection since. Amongst his best known tunes - classics they have become in his own sphere - are the *Bonnie Lass o' Bon Accord*, the *Miller o' Hirn, Music o' Spey, Glenlivet, Fyvie Castle*, and *Flower o' the Quern*.

A Cameo

One cameo of Scott Skinner, the musician and the man, may be drawn. Arm-and-arm with a friend, he was walking along Market Street, Aberdeen, one day, when his quick ear caught the strains of a familiar air somewhat feebly wailed out on a decrepit violin played by an old man. The friend felt he hand of Scott Skinner twitch upon his arm and then loosen its grip. The Strathspey King crossed into Hadden Street, and addressing the old man in the vernacular, said, "Lat's see your fiddle, laddie." The "laddie" looked quite ten years the senior of the "King," and very infirm at that. A momentary tuning up of the instrument followed, and then came welling out the ear-haunting phrases of *The Lass o' Bon Accord*, presented as none else could. "There," addressing the street musician, and handing back the fiddle, "that's the way to play that tune, and I should ken, for"—with a gratified inflection of the voice that gave richness to its tone—"it was me that made it."

Romantic Presence

Aberdonians will long remember his romantic-looking presence. A portrait of him, presented at a great Burns concert in Edinburgh ten years ago, is in Dundee Art Gallery. Mr Scott Skinner was twice married, and his widow resides abroad. A son by the first marriage, Mr Manson Scott Skinner, settled in Australia, and served in the war with the Anzacs.

—Aberdeen Evening Express 17.3.1927

Strathspey King's Burial

Pipers Head Cortege

Crowds on Route to Allenvale

THOUSANDS OF PEOPLE, mostly womenfolk, witnessed the funeral of Mr James Scott Skinner, the "Strathspey King," of violin playing fame, as the cortege passed through the streets of Aberdeen on its way from his residence, 25 Victoria Street, to Allenvale Cemetery on Saturday afternoon. A service was conducted in the house by Rev J.J.S.Thomson, M.C.,M.A., John Knox Parish Church, in presence of a few relatives and friends, and the oak coffin, bearing the simple inscription: *James Scott Skinner, aged 84 years,* was then bourne to the hearse. On the coffin was placed Mr Scott Skinner's violin in open case, draped in black, and a number of beautiful floral tributes, one of them representing a fiddle with a broken string, and another a harp.

Public's Last Tribute

Preceded by the kilted City Police Pipe Band under Pipe-Major Sergt. Henderson and Drum-Major Constable David Ross, the cortege moved slowly off to the plaintive lament *Flowers o' the Forest.* The hearse was followed by about 30 mourners and half-a-dozen motors. Victoria Street was lined with men, women, and children, and turning into Albyn Place the crowds on the pavement were two and three deep, while at Holburn Junction a striking scene was presented in the brilliant sunshine by the huge mass of spectators who, in reverent attitude, witnessed the passing of the noted Scottish violinist, whose fiddle, a conspicuous object on the coffin, had so often stirred their emotions. The men raised their hats and many of the women were in tears.

All along Holburn Street the crowd was so dense that the vehicular traffic was held up at one point and their were similar manifestations of public interest as the cortege moved into Fonthill Road and down Whinhill Road, towards the cemetery, the slow march still being made to the strains of the *Flowers o' the Forest.*

The place of burial was close to the main entrance of the cemetery, and a large crowd assembled to witness the last rites. The coffin was carried to the graveside from the hearse, and after the fiddle and flowers had been removed, the remains were lowered by the pall-bearers, the Rev Mr Thomson uttering the words—"Earth to earth, and dust to dust." He then offered prayer, in which occurred the sentence—"We thank Thee for the life, work, and character of the departed. We thank thee for his great musical talent, and for the health and strength which enabled him to develop that talent, and we thank Thee that he was able to influence for good thereby thousands of fellow men."

Lochaber No More

The touching obsequies concluded with the playing of the lament, *Lochaber No More*, by Mr George S. M'Lennan, formerly of the Gordon Highlanders, and as the appealing strains died away and all that was mortal of the "Strathspey King" was committed to the last resting-place, many of the mourners and spectators were deeply affected.

The pall-bearers were:- Mr Thomas Dalgarno, Aberdeen (nephew); Mr James M'Donald, Allenvale (cousin); Mr M'Millan, Glasgow; Mr Alex. Sim, Aberdeen; Mr Alex. Simpson, Aberdeen Savings Bank; Sergeant M'Millan, depot, Gordon Highlanders; Mr Harry Gordon, Beach Pavilion; Mr Chas. Sutherland, Fraserburgh.

The general company included Sir James Taggart, Messrs. Jas. F. Donald, George Strathdee, Wm. Kemp, George Rettie, James Morrison, W. Paull, John Pirie, J. Henderson, Jas. Dickie, New Deer; Ewan, Banchory; John Knowles, Ballater; Gavin M'Lennan, Glasgow; Slorach, Bucksburn; A. and W. Strachan, Aberdeen; John Davidson, W. Glennie, John Kennedy, Robert Garrow, fish merchant; W.C. Forbes, solicitor; C.S. France.

Wreaths were sent by Mr Stuart (brother-in-law), Mrs Stuart and family, Viewfield, Aberlour; the Musical Trade Profession and Friends; Mrs Richards and family, 25 Victoria Street; the Glasgow Caledonian Strathspey and Reel Society; Mr John M'Hardy, London; the M'Ewan family, Banchory; Mr and Mrs C. Sutherland, Fraserburgh; Myrtle, Veronica and John North, 25 Victoria Street; Mrs Violet Thomson Pyper, Oakhill Road; Miss Jeannie Hendry, 15 Albyn Place; Mr J. Lawrence, Aberdeen; Mrs Morris, 12a Mount Street; Mr and Mrs Donaldson, Westside Cottage, Newmachar.

—Aberdeen Journal 21.3.1927

Pipe-Major G. S. M'Lennan, late of the Gordon Highlanders, played the lament *Lochaber No More* at the graveside of the Strathspey King in Allenvale Cemetery.

Funeral cortege of the late Mr J. Scott Skinner, headed by the Aberdeen City Police pipers, turning Albyn Place from Victoria Street.

GRAND SCOTCH
ENTERTAINMENTS.

MECHANICS' HALL, 6th JULY.

The BROTHERS SKINNER beg to submit the following Programme for Public patronage :—

ARTISTES.

Mr J. SEDGEWICK BATTIE,
Scotch Vocalist, Pianist, Violinist, &c., Aberdeen.

MISS B. E. ROY,
(From Breda—Twelve Years of Age.)

MISS ISABELLA BREMNER,
(From Alford—Nine Years of Age.)

Mr. A. F. SKINNER, (late of the 79th Cameron Highlanders),
VIOLINIST AND DANCER—Deeside. (First appearance for 12 Years.)

MASTER JOHN BREMNER,
(From Alford—Six Years of Age.)

MASTER C. B. FORBES,
(From Strathdon—Twelve Years of Age.)

MASTER J. R. LEITH,
(From Glenkindy—Champion Fling Dancer.)

MR. JAMES SCOTT SKINNER,
LEADER AND VIOLIN SOLOIST,
(FOR SIX YEARS A PUPIL OF THE LATE DR. MARK.)
Banchory, Deeside.

PROGRAMME.

Part First.

OVERTURE......" Guy Mannering," (Sir H. R. Bishop)...... PIANOFORTE & SELECT BAND.

SONG......................" M'Crimman's Lament,"..............................Mr. BATTIE

Is your war-pipe asleep, and for ever, M'Crimman ?
Is your pipe asleep, and for ever ?
Shall the pibroch that welcomed the foe to Benaar,
Be hush'd when we seek the dark wolf in his lair,
To give back our wrongs to the giver ?
To the raid and the onslaught our chieftains have gone,
Like the course of the fire-draught their clanmon passed on
With the lance and the shield 'gainst the foe they have bound
them,
And have ta'en to the field with their vassals around them.

Then raise your wild slogan-cry ! On to the foray !
Sons of the heather-hill, pine-wood and glen !
Shout for M'Pherson, M'Leod, and the Moray,
Till the Lomonds re-echo the challenge again.

Youth of the daring heart, bright be thy doom,
As the bodings which light up thy bold spirit now ;
But the fate of M'Crimman is closing in gloom,
And the breath of the grey wraith hath passed o'er his brow :
Victorious in joy thou'lt return to Benaar,
And be clasped to the hearts of thy best beloved there ;
But M'Crimman, M'Crimman, M'Crimman, never, never, never,
never.

Wilt thou shriek from the doom thou canst shun not, M'Crim-
man ?
Wilt thou shrink from the doom thou canst shun not ?
If thy course must be brief, let the proud Saxon know,
That the soul of M'Crimman ne'er quail'd when a foe
Bared his blade in the land he had won not !
Where the light-footed roe leaves the wild breeze behind,
And the red heather bloom gives its sweets to the wind,
There our broad pennon flies, and the keen steeds are prancing,
'Mid the startling war-cries, and the war weapons glancing.

Then raise your wild slogan-cry ! On to the foray !
Sons of the heather hill, pine-wood and glen !
Shout for M'Pherson, M'Leod and the Moray,
Till the Lomonds re-echo the challenge again.

VIOLIN SOLO, with variations......................................Mr. J. S. SKINNER.

GHILLIE CALLUM..Master C. B. FORBES.

COMIC SONG (in character)........................... ... .Mr F. LINN
                                                          Mr. A. F. SKINNER,
REEL O' THUILLEACHAN, with variations,.....................
                    (Late 79th Cameron Highlanders.)   PUPILS.

DANCE......................." Reel o' Thuilleachan,".............MR. A. F. SKINNER.

Grand Selection of Strathspeys and Reels,

Composed by the Brothers SKINNER,

Including Sir Alexander Anderson's Strathspey ; Lady Anderson's Reel , Miss Neil's (Glenpatru)
Strathspey ; Granite City Reel ; Howe of Echt ; A. Symon's Reel (Netherley Postman.)

SCOTCH HORNPIPE............" Mrs. Benton of Airlie,"............Mr. A. F. SKINNER.

Part Second.

QUADRILLE ON SCOTCH AIRS......" Ettrick Vale"......PIANOFORTE & SELECT BAND.
                                Composed by J. S. SKINNER.

HIGHLAND FLING...................................Master J. BREMNER (6 years of age.)

SONG................." Go Fetch to Me a Pint o' Wine,"................Mr. BATTIE

Go fetch to me a pint o' wine,
    And fill it in a silver tassie,
That I may drink, before I go,
    A service to my bonnie Lassie
The boat rocks at the pier o' Leith,
    And keen the wind blaws frae the ferry,
The ship rides by the Berwick Law,
    And I maun leave my bonnie Mary.
        Go fetch to me, &c.

The trumpets sound, the banners fly,
    The glitt'ring spears are ranked ready,
The shouts o' war, are heard afar,
    The battle closes thick and bloody ;
But it's not the roar o' sea or shore,
    Would mak' me langer wish to tarry,
Nor shouts o' war that's heard afar,
    It's leaving thee my bonnie Mary.
        Go fetch to me, &c.

LOSSACH HIGHLAND FLING....................................Mr. A. F. SKINNER.
                    In full Highland Costume.

VIOLIN SOLO,................." Gems of Scotland,"............Mr. J. S. SKINNER.

HIGHLAND FLING..PUPILS.

SWORD DANCE..Mr. J. S. SKINNER.

SCOTCH MEDLEY..Miss BREMNER

SONG......................" Jessie's Dream,"............................Mr. BATTIE.

HIGHLAND FLING...

COMIC SONG...Mr F. LINN

FIRST PRIZE TUNES,

Inverness Competition, 1863.

GAINED BY MR JAMES SCOTT SKINNER

Mr. A. F. SKINNER will play his

Prize Tunes which Gained him the Purse of Sovereigns

At the Edinburgh Competition, 1866.

Scott Skinner

A Friend's Estimate

NOW THAT SCOTT SKINNER has gone, and will no more delight us with his magic strains, it may not be amiss for one who knew him well, who admired his gifts, and recognised his limitations, to try to indicate where he stood as an exponent and composer of Scottish music.

In matters of this kind there is usually room for differences of opinion; but the present writer desires it to be understood that he has no wish to indulge in extreme statements, or to give expression to opinions which are not in some degree susceptible to proof.

As a player of Strathspeys and reels, Skinner stood in a class by himself. The verve and spirit, the faultless rhythm, the wonderful bowing and fingering, and not least, the poetic fervour which characterised his playing of these effusions will not readily be forgotten. His was the last word in Strathspey playing, and his influence has been so great that he may almost be said to have founded a new school. Contrary to what many believe, there are probably more Strathspey players of merit to- day than at any former time, due in great measure to Skinner's teaching and example. And lastly, although his love centred chiefly in Scottish music, he could when he so desired, give a perfectly good account of himself in music of a quite different kind.

How then does Skinner as a violinist compare with Niel Gow and other noted fiddlers of the past? The estimation in which Niel (that is how he spelt his name) was held during his life, and the many testimonies to his abilities which have come down to us, prove that he was considered to be far in advance of his contemporaries. Time instead of diminishing his fame, has only added to it, till now there has gathered around his name a mass of legend against which argument is powerless.

Niel Gow's Limitations

Granting Niel Gow's natural abilities, when we consider that he was mainly self-taught, and keep in view the great advance that has taken place in violin playing since his day, is it natural to suppose that he was anything like equal to Skinner with similar natural endowments, combined with a technique which, it is safe to assume, Gow never possessed? A number of years ago the matter was thus disposed of by a Buchan bard:-

I've aft been tauld hoo aul Niel Gow
Could gar his elbock diddle, O.
Hoo Marshall and hoo Daniel Dow
Could play upon the fiddle, O;
But were they a' placed in a raw
Te play alang wi' Skinner, O,
He'd let you see, in meenits three,
Wha wad come aff the winner, O.

Skinner was a prolific composer of fiddle music. Besides many single sheets, he issued no fewer than five Collections, the last being *The Harp and Claymore*, his magnum opus. While justifiably proud of his playing, his greatest desire was to be known and remembered as a composer, not only of Strathspeys and reels, but of other classes of music as well. It is purely as a Strathspey composer, however, that he has to be considered.

Those who are familiar with the structure of the Strathspey know that there is a point beyond which it cannot be developed without losing its character. That point had already been reached before the coming of Skinner, by the Gows, Marshall, and others. It is not for the Strathspey composer to disport himself among the various keys, or indulge in fanciful chromatic progressions. In spite of all this he managed to impart a general character to his tunes which differentiates them from those of an older date. The best of them are robust, melodious, and exceptionally well balanced. As a composer he shows more versatility than Gow; but, on the whole, lacks the charm and spontaneity of Marshall. He often said that the only tune he ever envied anyone was *The Marquis of Huntly's Farewell.*

One of the most popular, and certainly the most original, of all his Strathspey tunes is the *Miller o' Hirn.* It has a character and individuality of its own, and may likely continue to be heard when many of the others are forgotten. Among the best may be mentioned *Glenlivet, Forbes Morrison—* dainty tune—*Tulchan Lodge, The Laird o' Drumblair,* and in a different style, *Mrs Farquharson of Whitehouse.* His reels, though open to the objection of sameness, have a vivacity and sprightliness very characteristic of their author, and are by no means easy to play.

Musical Snobbery

Like other Strathspey composers of note, he admittedly wrote too much, and repeated himself again and again. As has already been said, his work both as a player and composer, combined with that of the late Peter Milne of Aberdeen, did much to revive interest in Strathspey playing, which had greatly declined, more by reason of musical snobbery than anything else. What place he will ultimately occupy among Strathspey composers time alone can determine.

He was not successful as a composer of song airs, with one or two exceptions, or slow airs generally. *Bovaglie's Plaid* may be taken as one of the exceptions. Such tunes as *The Cradle Song, Flower o' the Quern,* and *The Duchess Tree* are merely puerile and should never have been printed. He had but a slight knowledge of harmony, and usually depended on others to supply his accompaniments. Still, when all is said, it may be safely assumed that no one with equal gifts will ever devote himself exclusively to the cultivation of Scottish music, which makes it tolerably certain that in his own particular walk "We ne'er shall look upon his like again."

It may be stated in conclusion that the foregoing has been written in fulfilment of a promise exacted from the writer years ago by the "Strathspey King" himself.

—George Riddell
Aberdeen Journal 27.4.1927

MR. ROSE WOOD'S
GRAND
Evening Concert
AND
𝕰xhibition of 𝕯ancing,

Town Hall, Elgin,

WEDNESDAY, 16TH APRIL 1919.

Artistes—

Mr. SCOTT SKINNER	- The Strathspey King
Miss BESSIE GIBSON	- - - Soprano
Mr. WILLIE KEMP	- - - Comedian

Mr. ROSE WOOD'S PUPILS

Pianist and Accompanist   -   -   Mrs. SHAND

Doors open at 7.30; Early Door to Ticketholders, 7.15;
Concert at 8 o'clock.

Admission (including Tax): Reserved Seats, 3/6;
Second Seats, 2/4; Third Seats, 1/3.

PROGRAMMES 2D. EACH.

PROGRAMME.

Pianoforte Selection	... ...	Mrs. SHAND	
Dance	... "Continental Boston"	Misses Ruby Ewen and Nettie Duncan	
Dance	... "Highland Fling"	Miss Aurora Reid	
Dance	... "La Reine Gavotte"	Misses Jean Russell and Constance Winchester	
Song	... "Good Bye" ... ... *Tosti*	Miss Bessie Gibson	
Dance	... "Sword Dance"	Miss Annie Grant	
Dance	... "Fox Trot"	Misses Jean Russell and Constance Winchester	
Song	... "I'm a Happy Married Man"	Mr. Willie Kemp	
Dance	... "Highland Reel"	Misses Annie Grant, Aurora Reid, Janet Bone, and Margaret Mackenzie	
Dance	... "Three-Step"	Misses Nettie Duncan and Ruby Ewen	
Pastoral Idyll	"Warblings from the Hills" ... *Skinner*	Mr. Scott Skinner	

Introducing: The Flowers o' the Forest—The Braes o' Auchtertyre—The Bonnie Lass o' Bon Accord—The Athole Highlanders' Farewell to Loch Katrine—The Marquis of Huntly's Farewell (Strathspey)—The Marquis of Tullibardine (Reel)—and Maggie Lauder

Dance	... ... "Irish Jig"	Miss Aurora Reid	
Dance	... ... "The Jazz"	Misses Ruby Ewen and Nettie Duncan	
Dance	... ... "Shean Truibhais"	Miss Annie Grant	
Song	... ... "Lochnagar"	Miss Bessie Gibson	
Dance	... "Gavotte Fox Trot"	Misses Constance Winchester and Ruby Ewen	
Dance	... ... "Sailor's Hornpipe"	Misses Aurora Reid and Annie Grant	
Song	... "Why do the Men Run After Me" ...	Mr. Willie Kemp	
Dance	... ... "Skirt Dance"	Miss Aurora Reid	
Dance	... ... "French Gavotte"	Miss Annie Grant	
Heroic Idyll	... "Spey's Furies" ... *Skinner*	Mr. Scott Skinner	

Introducing: Bovaglie's Plaid—The Gay Gordons—The Cameron Highlanders—The Laird o' Drumblair—Gladstone Reel—Mrs. Scott Skinner—The Miller o' Hirn—and The Spey in a Spate

Dance	... ... "Tickle Toe"	Misses Constance Winchester and Ruby Ewen	
Dance	... ... "Reel o' Tuilleachan"	Misses Aurora Reid, Annie Grant, Janet Bone, and Margaret Mackenzie	

124

The "Strathspey King"

£78 Realised for Violin at Auction

AN HEIRLOOM of a well-known Speyside family, and the musical treasure of the last of the great Scottish Strathspey fiddlers, the violin of the late Mr James Scott Skinner passed into the hands of an Aberdeen violin maker yesterday afternoon for £78 in a public roup in the garden at the rear of the house in Victoria Street in which the "Strathspey King" spent the last years of his life.

The Highland dress suit invariably adorned the dapper figure of the great fiddler when he was charming audiences with his music in theatre or dance hall was the first article to be disposed of. The suit consisted of a tunic, white vest and lace collar, kilt, plaid, stockings, and buckled brogues. There was no competition, and the first offer of £2 had to be accepted, the purchaser being Mrs Richards, broker.

The silver-mounted sporran, dirk, skean dhu, powder horn, and two Cairgorm brooches, were all disposed of to one purchaser. One of the dress brooches fetched £4 12s 6d, and the other £2 2s 6d, while the sporran sold at £2 17s 6d, the dirk at £2 15s, the powder horn at £2 12s 6d, and the skean dhu at £1 17s 6d.

When the auctioneer, Mr G. M. Cameron, lifted the favourite violin from the wooden case, which bore the inscription on a silver plate, "Presented to Mr James Scott Skinner by Mr William Grant, of Elchies and Carron, 1873," the intending purchasers pressed round the auctioneers chair, trampling underfoot the garden flowers in their eagerness to get a glimpse of the instrument that had earned for Mr Scott Skinner a wide reputation as a player of Strathspeys. The violin, which was an heirloom in the family of Mr William Grant, was presented to the "Strathspey King," by Mr Grant while Mr Skinner was giving dancing lessons to the young people of Carron and district in 1873.

Bidding was slow. The opening offer was £40, and two competitors carried the price to the region of £75 when Mr A. Strachan, violin maker, Belmont Street, Aberdeen outbid his rival by a small sum to get the fiddle at £78. Mr A. Strachan was acting on behalf of a south-country client, whose name was not divulged, but it is understood that the violin will remain in Scotland.

—Aberdeen Journal 7.5.1927

---

25 VICTORIA STREET.

IMPORTANT SALE OF HOUSEHOLD FURNITURE
AND
Personal Effects belonging to the late Mr James Scott Skinner,
On FRIDAY, 6th May, at 2.30 p.m. prompt.
The Sale will include:—
Mr SKINNER'S FAMOUS VIOLIN (gifted to him in 1873 by Wm. Grant, Esq. of Elchies and Carron), HIGHLAND DRESS SUIT, SILVER - MOUNTED SPORRAN, DIRK, SKEAN-DHU, POWDER HORN, and DRESS BROOCH—all fitted with Cairngorm Stones; Unique Set of Table Knives, Forks, and Carvers, mounted with Deer Horn Handles; Plated Inkstand, Gurkha Knife, Electro-Plate Spirit Kettle and Stand, Set of 4 Inlaid Mahogany Chairs, Inlaid Mahogany Table, Lacquer Wall Mirror, 2ft. 6in. Mahogany Bureau, 5ft. Carved Oak Table, Welsh Dresser, 3ft. Wardrobe, Couch, Dressing Chest, Bedsteads, Chairs, Toilet ware, Japanese Decorated China Tea Set, All-Brass Kerb and Dogs, Carpet, Rugs, Linoleum, Blankets, Bolsters and Pillows, Pictures, Chair and Cushion Covers, Kitchen Utensils, etc., etc.

NOTE.—Mr Skinner's Violin and other Personal Articles will be exposed for Sale at 3.30 p.m.
On View Morning of Sale from 10 o'clock.
GEO. M. CAMERON,
12 Justice Mill Lane.   Auctioneer and Valuator.
'Phone, 1168.

Late Scott Skinner

Move to Erect A Memorial to Violinist

MR GEORGE WALKER, the well-known Aberdeen entertainer, who recently returned to his native town after a prolonged absence in South Africa, Australia, and New Zealand, has found an immediate response to his appeal for the erection of a memorial to the late Mr J. Scott Skinner, the "Strathspey King," whose skill with the violin and as a composer, entitled him to be ranked as one of Scotland's musical geniuses. Mr Walker was surprised to find when he went to visit Mr Scott Skinner's grave in Allenvale that there was no public memorial.

Ready Response

Letters from all parts of the country have been received by Mr Walker in support of his appeal, and several handsome donations have already been forwarded.

To put the movement on a proper footing it is necessary to have a properly constituted representative committee, and several prominent ladies and gentlemen are being approached by Mr Walker with the object of enlisting their sympathy and services. Miss Violet Davidson, formerly of the Beach Pavilion, has written to Mr Walker, with a donation of five guineas, and Miss Jeannie Hendry has sent a similar sum. Mr Walker himself has contributed £5.

There are a great many admirers of the late Mr Scott Skinner's music and his playing in Scotland, particularly in the north, and it is believed that when the committee is formed and an appeal made for funds to erect a memorial, there will be a generous response.

Letter to London Scots

Mr Walker is having a letter sent to Mr John Douglas, head of the Caledonian Scots in London, and will approach the Lord Provost to act as chairman of the committee and get the Town Council to lend its patronage to any function that may be arranged. From London there have been inquiries as to what is intended to be done, and Mr Walker later on will let all interested know the position and the steps being taken in connection with the memorial.

Miss Violet Davidson associates herself whole-heartedly with the project for a memorial to Mr Scott Skinner, and writes that she is sure there are many friends of the "old warrior" who only want an opportunity to show their appreciation in some tangible form to make the appeal for funds a complete success.

—Aberdeen Evening Express 9.8.1930

126

After unveiling the memorial to Scott Skinner in Allenvale Cemetery, Aberdeen, on Saturday, Sir Harry Lauder placed a wreath as a tribute to the departed composer and violinist.

PROGRAMME OF
J. SCOTT SKINNER'S
FAREWELL

CARNIVAL

AND

Re=Union of Friends and Pupils

MUSIC HALL, ABERDEEN,

29th October, 1886.

ADMISSION 2/- & 1/-

DOORS OPEN AT 7 P.M.
COMMENCE AT 7.30.

Printed at the Adelphi Press by Taylor & Henderson, Music Printers, &c.